A Routledge Literary Sourcebook on

Harriet Beecher Stowe's
Uncle Tom's Cabin

First published in book form in 1852, *Uncle Tom's Cabin* quickly became a best-seller, recognized as a powerful contribution to antislavery debates. After more than 150 years, it remains one of the most widely discussed works of American literature, with critics focusing on a broad range of issues from abolition and racism to domesticity and Christian charity.

This Routledge Literary Sourcebook begins with a section on Contexts, which sets the novel in its cultural contexts and examines the life and career of Harriet Beecher Stowe. In this section the editor also reprints and comments upon important documents from the period, including relevant letters, poems by Frances Harper and excerpts from Stowe's later *Key to Uncle Tom's Cabin*. The Sourcebook's second section, Interpretations, offers a survey of criticism of the book from publication to the present, as well as extracts from reviews and key critical texts. It also touches upon dramatic interpretations of the novel. The following section, Key Passages, provides selected extracts from the novel, which are lucidly introduced and linked to the contextual and critical materials elsewhere in the Sourcebook. The volume is completed by suggestions for Further Reading.

Bringing together a wealth of material with clear critical commentary, Debra J. Rosenthal offers the ideal starting point for anyone studying this crucial American novel.

Debra J. Rosenthal is Assistant Professor of English at John Carroll University in Cleveland, Ohio. Her previous publications include *The Serpent in the Cup: Temperance in American Literature* (co-edited with David Reynolds, 1997), and *Mixing Race, Mixing Culture: Inter-American Literary Dialogues* (co-edited with Monika Kaup, 2002).

Routledge Literary Sourcebooks

Series Editor: Duncan Wu, St Catherine's College, Oxford University

A Routledge Literary Sourcebook on

Harriet Beecher Stowe's *Uncle Tom's Cabin*

Edited by Debra J. Rosenthal

Routledge
Taylor & Francis Group

NEW YORK AND LONDON

First published 2004

Simultaneously published in the UK, USA and Canada
by Routledge
29 West 35th Street, New York, NY 10001
and Routledge
11 New Fetter Lane, London EC4P 4EE

Routledge is an imprint of the Taylor & Francis Group

Editorial matter and selection © 2004 Edited by Debra J. Rosenthal

Typeset in Sabon and Gill Sans by RefineCatch Limited, Bungay, Suffolk
Printed and bound in Great Britain by
TJ International Ltd, Padstow, Cornwall

Library of Congress Cataloging in Publication Data
A Routledge literary sourcebook on Harriet Beecher Stowe's Uncle
Tom's cabin /c edited by Debra J. Rosenthal.
     p.   cm. – (Routledge literary sourcebooks)
Includes bibliographical references and index.
1. Stowe, Harriet Beecher, 1811–1896. Uncle Tom's cabin.   2. Didactic
fiction, American – History and criticism.   3. Southern States – In
literature.   4. African Americans in literature.   5. Plantation life
in literature.   6. Slavery in literature.   I. Rosenthal, Debra J., 1964– .
II. Series.
  PS2954.U6R68   2003
  813'.3 – dc21   2003004907

British Library Cataloguing in Publication Data
A catalogue record for this book is available from the British Library

ISBN 0–415–23473–5 (hbk)
ISBN 0–415–23474–3 (pbk)

Contents

Modern Criticism 40

The Work in Performance 75

3: Key Passages

Introduction 81

Key Passages 82

4: Further Reading

Series Editor's Preface

The Routledge Literary Sourcebook series has been designed to provide students with the materials required to begin serious study of individual literary works, all in a single volume. This includes an overview of the critical history of the work, including extracts from important critical debates of recent decades, and a selection of key passages from the text itself. Volume editors provide introductory commentaries and annotation for the reader's guidance. These handy books provide almost everything most students will need for the contextual and critical overview of literature expected in schools and universities today.

This aim is reflected in the structure of each Sourcebook. Section 1, "Contexts," provides biographical data in the form of an author chronology and contemporary documents relating to the author and his or her work. In Section 2, "Interpretations," the editor assembles extracts from the most influential and important criticism throughout the history of the work. In some cases this includes materials relating to performances or adaptations. The third section, "Key Passages," gathers together the essential episodes from the literary text connected by editorial commentary and annotation so as to relate them to ideas raised earlier in the volume. The final section offers suggestions for further reading, including recommended editions and critical volumes.

Annotation is a key feature of this series. Both the original notes from the reprinted texts and new annotations by the editor appear at the bottom of the relevant page. The reprinted notes are prefaced with the author's name in square brackets, e.g. [Robinson's note.].

Routledge Literary Sourcebooks offer the ideal introduction to single literary works, combining primary and secondary materials, chosen by experts, in accessible form.

Duncan Wu

Acknowledgments

More than they know, the loving encouragement of Glenn, Nathaniel, and Ariana Starkman has been uplifting, selfless, and magical.

The Stowe-Day foundation in Hartford, Connecticut generously offered assistance during my visit there. I am extremely grateful to John Carroll University for awarding me a Summer Research Fellowship and two research assistance grants to complete this project. Joan Rosenthal ably proofread.

The wit, advice, and steady long-distance support of Duncan Wu, Liz Thompson, and Rosie Waters have been invaluable and sustaining.

The following publishers, institutions, and individuals have kindly given permission to reprint materials:

CAMBRIDGE UNIVERSITY PRESS, for J. F. Yellin, "Doing it Herself: *Uncle Tom's Cabin* and Woman's Role in the Slavery Crisis," in *New Essays on Uncle Tom's Cabin*. Published by Cambridge University Press, 1986; Lawrence Buell, *New England Literary Culture: From Revolution through Renaissance*. Published by Cambridge University Press, 1986.

JOHNS HOPKINS UNIVERSITY PRESS, for Cynthia Griffin Wolff, "Masculinity in *Uncle Tom's Cabin*," *American Quarterly*, 47:4 (1995), © The American Studies Association. Reprinted by permission of the Johns Hopkins University Press; Jim O'Loughlin, "Articulating Uncle Tom's Cabin," *New Literary History*, 31:3 (2000), 580–2. © The University of Virginia. Reprinted by permission of the Johns Hopkins University Press.

MODERN LANGUAGE ASSOCIATION, for Marianne K. Noble, "Masochistic Eroticism in *Uncle Tom's Cabin*," in *Approaches to Teaching Stowe's Uncle Tom's Cabin*, 2000.

OXFORD UNIVERSITY PRESS, for Jane Tompkins, *Sensational Designs: The Cultural Work Of American Fiction 1790–1860*, © 1985 by Oxford University Press, Inc. Used by permission of Oxford University Press, Inc.

UNIVERSITY OF CALIFORNIA JOURNALS, for Peter Stoneley, 'Sentimental Emasculations: *Uncle Tom's Cabin* and *Black Beauty*," *Nineteenth-Century*

Literature 54/1 (1999). Reprinted by permission of the Regents of the University of California © 1999.

UNIVERSITY OF CALIFORNIA PRESS, for Amy Lang, *Prophetic Woman: Anne Hutchinson and the Problem of Dissent in the Literature of New England*, 1987; Gillian Brown, *Domestic Individualism: Imagining Self in Nineteenth-Century America*, 1990.

UNIVERSITY OF TEXAS PRESS, for Susan Gillman, "The Squatter, the Don, and The *Grandissimes* in Our America," in *Mixing Race, Mixing Culture: Inter-American Literary Dialogues* edited by Monika Kaup and Debra J. Rosenthal, 2002.

The publishers have made every effort to contact copyright holders. Any omission brought to our attention will be rectified in future editions.

Introduction

The city map of Hartford, Connecticut that car rental companies hand out to their clients clearly indicates many highlights of the city: the State Capitol building, the Supreme Court of the state of Connecticut, Trinity College, and the University of Hartford. As well, the map directs tourists to the home of one of its famous residents: the map marks the location of the Mark Twain house. Yet the map does not mark the location of the home of Twain's next-door neighbor, a writer whose most famous book outsold those of Twain and who went on to become the best-selling writer of the nineteenth century: Harriet Beecher Stowe (1811–96). A visitor to Hartford could easily miss the Stowe house and museum, yet it would be hard to miss seeing the city's glossy promotional brochure entitled "Mark Twain's Hartford." In fact, literary critic Jane Tompkins noted that when she lived in Hartford, Connecticut in 1969, before the rise of the women's movement, she visited the Mark Twain house but ignored the Harriet Beecher Stowe house (see her essay in this volume **pp. 42–7**). It is lamentable that more than thirty years later Stowe remains in Twain's shadow in this city.

The map's failure to include Stowe's house emblematizes Stowe's status until recently in the literary canon: her works stood in the shadow of male writers. Until about twenty-five years ago, *Uncle Tom's Cabin* rarely appeared on university syllabi. Today, with the rediscovery and revaluation of women's writing, English courses now regularly include Stowe's works and scholarly articles on her fiction appear steadily in academic journals.

How could Harriet Beecher Stowe go from being internationally famous, the best-selling author of the nineteenth century whose best-known book was outsold only by the Bible, to a writer neglected in her own city? Literary tastes ebb and flow with the times, and early twentieth-century critics of U.S. literature believed Stowe's didacticism, sentimentality, and politics did not meet the intellectual and literary standards of such peers as Ralph Waldo Emerson, Henry David Thoreau, Nathaniel Hawthorne, Herman Melville, and Walt Whitman. Important twentieth-century African American critics, such as James Baldwin and Richard Wright, deride the novel as racist; indeed, the term "Uncle Tom" has come to refer unflatteringly to a black person overly servile or deferential to whites. However, Stowe's contribution to American literature is now undisputed, and her works, especially *Uncle Tom's Cabin*, enjoy great popularity. Indeed, students of American literature need to be conversant with *Uncle Tom's Cabin* in order to understand the rise and development of literature in the U.S.

First published in serial form in 1851 and then as a novel in 1852, *Uncle Tom's Cabin* is a work of moral urgency: it pleads with its readers to end slavery in the United States. Through its compelling story of the cruel suffering of the slave Uncle Tom as he is sold south deeper into slavery and the simultaneous escape north of the slave family of George, Eliza, and Harry Harris, the novel explores such issues as race, slavery, abolition, Christian belief, motherhood, national politics, child welfare, alcoholism, and the power of sentiment and tears.

Stowe's previous exclusion from the canon of important American works and her current centrality to a complete understanding of American literary maturity, in many ways reflect tensions inherent in her works. For example, as a white woman who advocated African American subjectivity, she nonetheless can be accused today of racist portrayals of blacks. While *Uncle Tom's Cabin* argues for the importance of women's voices and moral virtues, it nonetheless does not advocate that women gain political power or visibility – the novel seems at once to support and resist later feminist agendas. Also, the novel exhibits tensions between its seeming support for people of all classes and its class-bound endorsement of success and virtue. As well, the novel is at once deeply religious and yet highly critical of the church's explicit and implicit support of slavery.

This Sourcebook provides a framework for understanding *Uncle Tom's Cabin*. The Contextual Overview section includes an introductory account of the chronology of Stowe's life and some of the documents published around the time *Uncle Tom's Cabin* first appeared. For example, an excerpt from a conduct manual written by Stowe's sister, reformer Catherine Beecher (1800–78), sheds light on early nineteenth-century beliefs about women's role in the home (**pp. 17–18**). Personal letters written by Stowe indicate how events of her life inspired much of the novel (**pp. 18–21**). The poetry of Frances Ellen Watkins Harper (1825–1911), perhaps the preeminent African American woman poet of the latter half of the nineteenth century, demonstrates the influence of *Uncle Tom's Cabin* on black poetic production (**pp. 21–4**).

In the Interpretations section, the Sourcebook includes early reviews of *Uncle Tom's Cabin* to give readers an idea of both the praise and the criticism the novel received. These are followed by extracts from modern criticism of *Uncle Tom's Cabin* – practically an industry unto itself. The sample extracts included here are linked to the Key Passages so that readers can make clear connections between the novel itself and the ways it has been interpreted by scholars and critics. Finally, information on the various dramatic interpretations of *Uncle Tom's Cabin* suggests to readers the powerful impact the novel had on the development of American theater.

The selection of Key Passages constitutes the major innovation of the Routledge Sourcebooks. Readers will find important passages from the novel annotated with plot summaries and linked to critical interpretations. Readers thus can get a sense of the novel as a whole as well as of many of the significant issues it raises.

Section 4, Further Reading, directs readers to other sources, both print and electronic, of information that can help enrich a study of *Uncle Tom's Cabin*.

1

Contexts

Contextual Overview

Harriet Beecher was born in Litchfield, Connecticut, on June 14, 1811 to Roxana Foote Beecher and Lyman Beecher, a Congregational minister. She was the seventh of what would be nine children.

When she was only five years old, Harriet's mother died, a devastating loss to the entire family. Although Harriet consequently did not have the advantage of a mother's guidance, she nonetheless received an excellent education: she enrolled at the Litchfield Female Academy when she was only eight, while most girls began to study at age twelve. Her sister Catherine became well known as an education reformer and started her own school, the Hartford Female Seminary. An excerpt from Catherine Beecher's *A Treatise on Domestic Economy* (1841) demonstrates her teachings, which placed women's moral excellence at the center of a successful home (**pp. 17–18**). Such teachings infuse *Uncle Tom's Cabin*'s characters Mrs. Bird and Rachel Halliday (Chapter 9 and Chapter 13), and indeed Harriet taught at Catherine's school from 1824 to 1832.

In 1832, at age twenty-one, Harriet Beecher moved from the established, cultured society of Litchfield to the then-primitive western town of Cincinnati, Ohio, when her father accepted a position as president of Lane Theological Seminary. For eighteen years she lived in a city just across the river from the slave-holding state of Kentucky, whose citizens were divided by opinion over whether to free the slaves or secede from the Union. Living among divided opinion allowed Harriet to assimilate ideas about race and slavery, ideas that would filter into her later writings.

The years in Cincinnati saw Harriet Beecher's rise as an author. She published her first stories there as well as a textbook, *Primary Geography for Children*. The textbook earned her an invitation to join the Semi-Colon Club, an exclusive literary society that provided Harriet with an audience. Club members met Monday evenings at 7:30 P.M. and an appointed member would read, unattributed, the works of the others. Discussion, refreshments, and dancing followed. One of Harriet's sketches, "Uncle Lot," won a contest sponsored by the *Western Monthly Magazine*. Her temperance story "Uncle Enoch" found a home back east in the *New-York Evangelist*. She continued to write regularly, especially sketches and short stories, and at the same time continued her teaching career by becoming an instructor at her sister Catherine's new school, the Western Female Institute.

It was also in Cincinnati that Harriet became a wife and mother. On January 6, 1836 she married Calvin Ellis Stowe, a clergyman and professor at Lane Seminary. The Protestant religion played an extremely significant role in Harriet Beecher's, and, from this point, Harriet Beecher Stowe's life. Her father had become famous as a Calvinist minister; her brother, Henry Ward Beecher, grew up to become an important preacher. She married a minister, and, later, she would become the mother of a minister. However, as a woman, Stowe was not permitted to become a minister herself nor to preach to a congregation. Also, as a woman, she found she could not accept her father's rigid patriarchal Calvinism. Some critics argue that Stowe's writings, and in particular *Uncle Tom's Cabin*, in effect became the pulpit from which she was allowed to speak. Her version of Christianity was to be more maternal-centered in that such selfless and nurturing characters as mothers, Uncle Tom, and Eva, prove to be saviors and the best interpreters of Christ's message.

By all accounts Harriet and Calvin's marriage seems to have been satisfying, but the seven children they had between 1836 and 1850 severely tried their relationship, finances, and Harriet's literary ambitions. The only effective means of birth control for them seemed to be long separations: Calvin often traveled abroad for months on business, and Harriet sought long, fashionable water-treatment cures at health spas.

Their first children, twins Hatty and Eliza, were born later in 1836, and their son Henry Ellis followed eighteen months later. Stowe continually felt challenged to be both a writer and a mother. Employing household help allowed her some time each day to devote to writing. As she wrote in a letter, "I have about three hours per day in writing & if you see my name coming out every where – you may be sure of one thing, that I *do* it for the *pay* – I have determined not to be a mere domestic slave." Stowe's use of the word "slave" to describe her possible fate rings with irony: one of her domestic workers turned out to be a slave whose mistress wanted to recapture her. The efforts of Calvin and Harriet's brother Henry to help the girl escape, driving her a dozen miles on back roads to a station on the Underground Railroad, provided Stowe with literary inspiration. The incident would become Eliza's dramatic escape in *Uncle Tom's Cabin*. While experiencing the joy at the births of her son Frederick in 1840, daughter Georgiana in 1843, and son Samuel Charles (Charley) in 1848, Stowe also suffered the sorrow of her brother George's suicide in 1843.

However, nothing compared to the suffering and sorrow over the death of baby Charley from cholera while Calvin was away, himself in weak health. In an 1852 letter to children's author Eliza Cabot Follen (**pp. 18–20**), Stowe linked her agony over Charley's death to the agony slave mothers feel when their children are sold away from them: "It was at *his* dying bed & at *his* grave, that I learnt what a poor slave mother may feel when her child is torn away from her." In many ways, the heart of *Uncle Tom's Cabin* lies at baby Charley's deathbed, for, as Stowe also wrote in the same letter, "[t]here were circumstances about his death, of such peculiar bitterness, of what might seem almost cruel suffering, that

I felt I could never be consoled for it, unless it should appear that this crushing of my own heart might enable me to work out some great good to others" (**p. 19**). In *Uncle Tom's Cabin* Stowe would turn her private grief into political action to save others from experiencing a similar grief.

In 1850, the year following baby Charley's death, Calvin accepted an offer to teach at Bowdoin College in Brunswick, Maine. Pregnant again, Harriet moved her household, while still writing and publishing, back to New England after eighteen years in Ohio. Some of her antislavery sketches appeared in the abolitionist weekly the *National Era*.

Sympathetic to the abolitionist cause, Stowe became outraged when Congress passed the Compromise of 1850 and the Fugitive Slave Law. The Compromise admitted California to the Union as a free state, but did not prohibit slavery in the New Mexico and Utah territories. The Fugitive Slave Law stated that anyone who fed, clothed, sheltered, or assisted an escaped slave could be jailed for six months and fined $1000. This law enraged many northerners. Up until that point, southern slave laws did not extend into the north, but from then on slave laws would affect northerners who wanted to show Christian charity to suffering slaves. One of Stowe's relatives encouraged her to "write something that will make this whole nation feel what an accursed thing slavery is."

That law, and a vision Stowe had in church of an old black slave being beaten, changed the course of her life and of American literature. Stowe's vision compelled her to pen what would become a literary and cultural phenomenon. Her son records that "Suddenly, like the unrolling of a picture, the scene of the death of Uncle Tom passed before her mind. So strongly was she affected that it was with difficulty she could keep from weeping aloud. Immediately on returning home she took pen and paper and wrote out the vision which had been as it were blown into her mind as by the rushing of a mighty wind."[1] When Stowe read the scene out loud to her family, they all wept together. Yet while the novel literally seems to have had a visionary beginning, Stowe also claimed that her novel fully represented real life. In a letter to Gamaliel Bailey (**pp. 20–1**), the editor of the *National Era*, she wrote that "My vocation is simply that of a *painter*, and my object will be to hold up in the most lifelike and graphic manner possible slavery, its reverses, changes, and the negro character."

Uncle Tom's Cabin, Or the Man That Was a Thing ran in the weekly Washington, D.C.-based moderate abolitionist newspaper the *National Era* for ten months, from the June 5, 1851 issue to the April 1, 1852 installment. Stowe received a great deal of fan mail as her audience steadily increased. When the novel was published in a two-volume book set in 1852 (with the subtitle *Life Among the Lowly*), it set new publishing records and sold out immediately. Harriet Beecher Stowe and *Uncle Tom's Cabin* became famous.

The half-decade from 1850–5, during which time Stowe published her great novel, has been dubbed the American Renaissance by critic F.O. Matthiessen

---

1   Charles Edward Stowe (ed.), *The Life of Harriet Beecher Stowe Compiled from Her Letters and Journals* (Boston: Houghton Mifflin, 1889), 148.

because of the number of major American works published during those five years. In his book *American Renaissance* (1941), Matthiessen noted that the years 1850–5 saw the publication of Ralph Waldo Emerson's *Representative Men* (1850), Nathaniel Hawthorne's *The Scarlet Letter* (1850) and *The House of the Seven Gables* (1851), Herman Melville's *Moby-Dick* (1851) and *Pierre* (1852), Henry David Thoreau's *Walden* (1854), and Walt Whitman's *Leaves of Grass* (1855).

Matthiessen did not include the best-selling novel of the nineteenth century, and, arguably, the century's most important novel, *Uncle Tom's Cabin*, in his book about important works that appeared in that critical half-decade. In fact, Matthiessen failed to include other best-selling women writers publishing during the same time period. For example, Susan Warner's *The Wide, Wide World* (1850) and Maria Cummins' *The Lamplighter* (1854) far outsold the works of Emerson, Hawthorne, Melville, Thoreau, and Whitman. Because of Matthiessen's omission, the literary accomplishments of Stowe and other women writers were denigrated for generations.

Why did Matthiessen only include Protestant white male writers from the northeast (and predominantly from Concord, Massachusetts) in his list of major authors? That question has kept scholars, especially feminist scholars, very active, for much work needs to be done to understand cultural biases against women and the narrative convention of sentiment. For example, feeling threatened by the success of such women writers as Stowe, Nathaniel Hawthorne wrote to his publisher in 1855, "America is now wholly given over to a damned mob of scribbling women, and I should have no chance of success while the public is occupied with their trash." Matthiessen seemed to share Hawthorne's anxiety, for he felt that his seminal book should only include the very best writers, and he chose to exclude Stowe and other women writers who also drew upon sentimental conventions (Jane Tompkins discusses biases against sentimentalism in her essay, **pp. 42–7**).

Although *Uncle Tom's Cabin* made Stowe famous, because of a disadvantageous royalty agreement, she did not become rich from book sales. Her family greatly needed what money she did earn from her writings, as Calvin's meager salary was not enough to support a wife and six children.

Once again Calvin's career forced the family to move, this time to Andover, Massachusetts. *Uncle Tom's Cabin* continued to sell vigorously, but many readers complained that they thought the novel falsely portrayed slavery. To document the veracity of her novel, Stowe wrote *A Key to Uncle Tom's Cabin*, which was published in 1853. In the Preface she wrote that "The writer has aimed, as far as possible, to say what is true, and only that, without regard to the effect which it may have upon any person or party" (see "Preface" to *A Key to Uncle Tom's Cabin*, on **pp. 24–5**). And she claimed the character of Uncle Tom was drawn from real life; in fact, she claimed to have based his character on Josiah Henson, a clergyman in Canada who escaped from slavery (see "Uncle Tom" from *A Key to Uncle Tom's Cabin*, on **pp. 25–6**).

The success of the novel led to Stowe touring England in 1854 and meeting with antislavery societies. The following year she published *Sunny Memories of*

Foreign Lands, which many Americans used as a guide book when they in turn sailed for Europe.

As we have seen, *Uncle Tom's Cabin* did not appear out of a void; a housewife and mother did not suddenly write a best-selling novel. Stowe had been writing for many years, especially sketches and short stories. After her success with *Uncle Tom's Cabin*, she continued to write: *Dred* (1856), *The Minister's Wooing* (1859), *The Pearl of Orr's Island* (1862), *Agnes of Sorrento* (1862), *Oldtown Folks* (1869), *Lady Byron Vindicated* (1870), *My Wife and I* (1871), *Pink and White Tyranny* (1871), *Oldtown Fireside Stories* (1872), and many others. Although not as politically galvanizing or as well known as *Uncle Tom's Cabin*, many of her later novels show her deft ear for her beloved New England region, her regard for her young female reading audience, and her valuation of women's domestic sphere.

In 1873 the Stowes moved to Forest Street in Hartford, Connecticut, next door to which Mark Twain would build his house the following year. It is here that Harriet wrote at least seven books and many short pieces, and here where, after fifty years of marriage, her husband Calvin died in 1886. After a decade-long decline in health, attended by her twin daughters, Harriet Beecher Stowe died in Hartford in 1896 at age eighty-five. Her house in Hartford is now a lovely museum filled with her actual furniture, paintings, and other items.

Chronology

1811

Harriet Beecher, born June 14 in Litchfield, Connecticut, the seventh of nine children of Congregational minister Lyman Beecher and Roxana Foote

1816

Roxana Foote dies from consumption at age forty-one

1819

Enters the Litchfield Female Academy at age eight, four years earlier than is usual

1824–32

Studies and becomes a teacher at the Hartford Female Seminary, a girls' school started by her older sister, reformist Catherine Beecher

1832

Lyman Beecher accepts the position of President of Lane Theological Seminary in Cincinnati, Ohio, then an unsophisticated frontier town divided by public opinion over abolition or secession from the Union; Beecher moves the established New England family west to what will be Harriet's home for the next eighteen years

1833

Harriet writes and publishes a textbook, *Primary Geography for Children*, which earns her an invitation to join the Semi-Colon Club, an exclusive literary society; essays and stories written for the Semi-Colons get published in the *Western Monthly Magazine*, and a sketch, "Uncle Lot," wins the magazine's contest and is published under the title "A New England Sketch"; teaches at her sister Catherine's new school, the Western Female Institute

1835

The *New-York Evangelist* publishes "Uncle Enoch," a temperance tale that draws upon her training as a schoolteacher to urge self-restraint with alcohol

1836

On January 6, marries Calvin Ellis Stowe, a professor at Lane Seminary in Cincinnati and a clergyman; in early June, with Harriet pregnant, Calvin sails from New York on a nine-month European trip, beginning in their marriage a pattern of long separations; Harriet gives birth to twins, Hatty and Eliza in Calvin's absence

1838

Son Henry Ellis is born; with three babies under eighteen months of age, Stowe employs two servants to do the housework and tend to the children so that she can write

1839

Calvin and Harriet's brother help the Stowes' domestic worker, legally a slave, to escape her mistress; incident will become Eliza's escape in *Uncle Tom's Cabin*

1840

Son Frederick is born

1843

Harriet's brother George, a reverend deeply concerned over doctrine of Christian perfectionism, commits suicide; daughter Georgiana is born, named after her dead brother; feeling helpless and flawed as a Christian, wife, and mother, experiences the "Victory" of sensing God's grace; continues to publish stories; selected New England tales are collected in *The Mayflower*

1846–7

Enjoys rest and recuperation by undergoing a "water cure" of healthy eating, exercise, and hydrotherapy at Brattleboro, Vermont

1848

Nine months after returning from the water cure, son Samuel Charles (Charley) is born; the healthiest and most contented baby Harriet has had, he is the only one she is well enough to nurse

1849

Little Charley dies from cholera

1850

Calvin accepts a teaching position at Bowdoin College in Brunswick, Maine; while Calvin finishes teaching at Lane Seminary, Harriet, six months pregnant, moves the family back to New England to organize the household before her husband joins them; Fugitive Slave Law passed by Congress; Harriet publishes antislavery sketches in the abolitionist weekly the

National Era; son Charles Edward, named after her dead baby Charley, is born

1851

Beginning in June, *Uncle Tom's Cabin* appears in serial form

1852

J.P. Jewett publishes *Uncle Tom's Cabin* in book form on March 20; family moves to Andover, Massachusetts, when Calvin accepts a position of professor of sacred literature; Stowe becomes a contributor to the *Independent*, an antislavery religious New York newspaper, until 1862

1853

Publishes *A Key to Uncle Tom's Cabin* to counter accusations that *Uncle Tom's Cabin* falsely portrays slavery; sails to England, where over a million copies of *Uncle Tom's Cabin* had been sold

1854

Publishes an essay to protest the Kansas–Nebraska Act, which would let Kansas and Nebraska decide whether they would be free or slave soil; publishes *Sunny Memories of Foreign Lands*, a travel book that Americans used as a tour guide when they visited Europe

1856

Publishes *Dred: A Tale of the Great Dismal Swamp*, another antislavery novel; tours Europe again

1857

Son Henry Ellis, a student at Dartmouth College, is pulled into a strong current while swimming in the Connecticut River and drowns

1859

Helps establish the *Atlantic Monthly* by serializing her first New England novel, *The Minister's Wooing*, which is then published in book form; third European tour

1862

Publishes her second New England novel, *The Pearl of Orr's Island*, and a novel of Italy, *Agnes of Sorrento*

1863

Calvin Stowe retires from Andover at age sixty-one, placing the burden of earning money on Harriet's pen; purchases "Oakholm," her first home in Hartford; meets President Lincoln, who reportedly suggests that Stowe helped initiate the Civil War by remarking to her, "so this is the little lady who made this big war"

1864

Recognizing that during the Civil War readers would be attracted to articles about the bliss and security of home life, Stowe writes a series of domestic essays for the *Atlantic Monthly*; published in book form the following year

1866

Invests in a cotton plantation in Florida for her son Fred, hoping that exercise, hard work, and limited temptations would steer this alcoholic, wayward son back towards a productive life; begins to make annual trips to Mandarin, Florida

1867

Publishes two volumes of children's stories and a collection of religious poems

1868

Publishes another collection of domestic essays and *Men of Our Times; or, Leading Patriots of the Day*

1869

Publishes a third New England novel, *Oldtown Folks*; publishes "The True Story of Lady Byron's Life," which exposes the poet Lord Byron's estrangement from his wife and his affair with his half-sister Augusta Leigh

1870

Publishes *Lady Byron Vindicated*, and more children's stories

1871

Unreformed, her son Fred disappears; publishes two novels: *My Wife and I* and *Pink and White Tyranny*

1872

Publishes *Oldtown Fireside Stories*; having sold "Oakholm" in 1870, Stowe purchases a new home on Forest Street in Hartford, Connecticut, next door to which Mark Twain will build his house

1873–84

Rich decade of publishing that sees the production of *Palmetto Leaves*, *Woman in Sacred History*, *We and Our Neighbors*, *Betty's Bright Idea*, *Footsteps of the Master*, *Poganuc People*, and *A Dog's Mission*

1886

After fifty years of marriage, her husband Calvin dies

1887

Daughter Georgiana, addicted to morphine, dies at age forty-four

1896

After a long decline in health, Harriet Beecher Stowe dies in Hartford on July 1 at age eighty-five

Contemporary Documents

From **Catherine Beecher, A Treatise on Domestic Economy** (1841)

> Harriet Beecher Stowe's sister, Catherine Beecher, was a leading advocate of women's education. Her 1841 book, A Treatise on Domestic Economy, addresses the many responsibilities a woman faced in running a home and rearing children. This excerpt shows women's, particularly mothers', moral strength and power to influence husbands, brothers, and children. In Chapter 9 of Uncle Tom's Cabin we see Mrs. Bird influencing her husband, Senator Bird (**pp. 89–96**), and in Chapter 13 (**pp. 99–104**) we see Rachel Halliday exemplifying Catherine Beecher's model. Jane Tompkins's essay (**pp. 42–7**) also draws upon women's moral superiority as articulated by Catherine Beecher.

[. . .] The success of democratic institutions, as is conceded by all, depends upon the intellectual and moral character of the mass of the people. If they are intelligent and virtuous, democracy is a blessing; but if they are ignorant and wicked, it is only a curse, and as much more dreadful than any form of civil government, as a thousand tyrants are more to be dreaded than one. It is equally conceded, that the formation of the moral and intellectual character of the young is committed mainly to the female hand. The mother writes the character of the future man; the sister bends the fibres that hereafter are the forest tree; the wife sways the heart, whose energies may turn for good or for evil the destinies of a nation. Let the women of a country be made virtuous and intelligent, and the men will certainly be the same. The proper education of a man decides the welfare of an individual; but educate a woman, and the interests of a whole family are secured.

If this could be so, as none will deny, then to American women, more than to any others on earth, is committed the exalted privilege of extending over the world those blessed influences, that are to renovate degraded man, and "clothe all climes with beauty."

No American woman, then, has any occasion for feeling that hers is an humble or insignificant lot. The value of what an individual accomplishes, is to be estimated by the importance of the enterprise achieved, and not by the particular position of the laborer. The drops of heaven that freshen the earth are each of equal value, whether they fall in the lowland meadow, or the princely parterre. The builders of a temple are of equal importance, whether they labor on the foundations, or toil upon the dome.

Thus, also, with those labors that are to be made effectual in the regeneration of the Earth. The woman who is rearing a family of children; the woman who labors in the schoolroom; the woman who, in her retired chamber, earns, with her needle, the mite to contribute for the intellectual and moral elevation of her country; even the humble domestic, whose example and influence may be moulding and forming young minds, while her faithful services sustain a prosperous domestic state; – each and all may be cheered by the consciousness, that they are agents in accomplishing the greatest work that ever was committed to human responsibility. [. . .]

From **letter to Eliza Cabot Follen**, December 16, 1852 from Joan Hedrick (ed.), *The Oxford Harriet Beecher Stowe Reader* (New York, N.Y.: Oxford University Press, 1999)

In this famous letter to American children's author Eliza Cabot Follen, Stowe briefly describes herself and her life. Most significantly, she relates how the death of her son Charley linked her to slave mothers whose children were sold away. Stowe believes that the heart of *Uncle Tom's Cabin* lies at the deathbed of her very young son.

Andover, Dec. 16/52

My Dear Madam,

I hasten to reply to your letter to me the more interesting that I have long been acquainted with you, and during all the nursery part of my life, made daily use of your little poems for children. I used to think sometimes in those days that I would write to you & tell you how much I was obliged to you for the pleasure which they gave us all.

So you want to know something about what sort of a woman I am – well, if this is any object, you shall have statistics free of charge.

To begin then, I am a little bit of a woman – somewhat more than 40 – about as thin & dry as a pinch of snuff – never very much to look at in my best days – & looking like a used up article now. I was married when I was 25 years old to a man rich in Greek & Hebrew, Latin & Arabic, & alas! rich in nothing else. When I went to housekeeping, my entire stock of china for parlour & kitchen was bought for 11 dollars, & this lasted very well for 2 years, till my brother who was married & brought in his bride to visit me & found upon review that I had neither plates nor teacups enough to set a table for my father's family, where-fore I thought it best to reinforce the establishment by getting me a tea-set which cost 10 dollars more, & this, I believe, formed my whole stock in trade for some years.

But then I was abundantly enriched with wealth of another kind. I had 2 little curly headed twin daughters to begin with, & my stock in this line has gradually increased till I have been the mother of 7 children, the most beautiful of which,[1] the most loved, lies buried near my Cincinnati residence. It was at *his* dying bed & at *his* grave, that I learnt what a poor slave mother may feel when her child is torn away from her. In the depths of sorrow, which seemed to me immeasurable, it was my only prayer to God that such anguish might not be suffered in vain! There were circumstances about his death, of such peculiar bitterness, of what might seem almost cruel suffering, that I felt I could never be consoled for it, unless it should appear that this crushing of my own heart might enable me to work out some great good to others. It was during the cholera summer, when in a circle of 5 miles around me, in the short space of 3 months, 9000 were buried around me, a mortality which I have never heard exceeded any where. My husband in feeble health was obliged to be absent the whole time, & I had sole charge of a family of 15 persons. He could not return to me because I would not permit it, for in many instances, where parents abroad had returned to their families in the infected atmosphere, the result had been sudden death, & the physicians warned me that if he returned it would be only to die. My poor Charley died for want of medical aid timely rendered for in the universal confusion & despair that prevailed, it was often impossible to obtain assistance till it was too late.

I allude to this now, because I have often felt that much that is in this book had its root in the awful scenes & bitter sorrows of that summer. It has left now, I trust, no trace in my mind except a deep compassion for the sorrowful, especially for mothers who are separated from their children. [. . .]

During these long years of struggling with poverty & sickness, & a hot debilitating climate, my children grew up around me. The nursery & the kitchen were my principal fields of labour.

Some of my friends pitying my toils, copied & sent some of my little sketches to certain liberally paying annuals, with my name. With the first money that I earned in this way, I bought a *feather bed*! for as I had married into poverty & without a dowry, & as my husband had only a large library of books, & a great deal of learning, this bed & pillows was thought on the whole, the most profitable investment. After this, I thought I had discovered the philosopher's stone, & when a new carpet or a mattress was going to be needed, or when at the close of the year, it began to be evident that my family accounts, like poor Dora's,[2] "*wouldn't add up*," then I used to say to my faithful friend & factotum Anna,[3]

---

1 A reference to her son Samuel Charles (Charley), 1848–9.
2 [Hedrick's note.] Dora Copperfield, the "child-wife" in Dickens's *David Copperfield*.
3 [Hedrick's note.] Anna Smith became Stowe's live-in household help in 1836, the year Stowe married and gave birth to twins. She stayed for the eighteen years of their Cincinnati, Ohio, sojourn, followed them to Brunswick, Maine, in 1850, and left shortly thereafter to return to the midwest.

who shared all my joys & sorrows, "Now if you'll keep the babies & attend to all the things in the house for one day, I'll write a piece, & then we shall be out of the scrape;" & so I became an authoress. [. . .]

You ask with regard to the remuneration which I have received for my work, here in America. Having been poor all my life, & expecting to be poor to the end of it, the idea of making anything by a book which I wrote just because I could not help it, never occurred to me. It was therefore, an agreeable surprise to receive ten thousand dollars as the first fruits of 3 months' sale. I presume as much more is now due. [. . .]

I suffer excessively in writing these things. It may truly be said I write with *heart's blood*. – Many times in writing "Uncle Tom's Cabin" I thought my health w^d fail utterly, but I prayed earnestly that God would help me till I got thro' – & now I am pressed above measure, & beyond strength – This horror, this nightmare, abomination! can it be in *my* country! It lies like lead on my heart, it shadows my life with sorrow, the more so, that I feel, as for my own brothers, for the South – & I am pained by every horror that I am obliged to write, as one who is forced by an awful oath, to disclose in a court, some family disgrace! Many times I have thought I must die, & yet, I pray God that I may live to see something done.

Yrs affectly
H. B. Stowe

Letter to Gamaliel Bailey, March 9, 1851 from Joan Hedrick (ed.), *The Oxford Harriet Beecher Stowe Reader* (New York, N.Y.: Oxford University Press, 1999)

In this letter to the editor of *National Era*, which would begin serializing *Uncle Tom's Cabin* three months after this letter was written, Stowe likens herself to a painter in order to emphasize that her novel realistically represents life. *Uncle Tom's Cabin*, Stowe therefore claims, will impress its readers/viewers with unassailable images of slavery and slaves.

Brunswick, March 9 [1851]
Maine

Mr. Bailey,
Dear Sir:

I am at present occupied upon a story which will be a much longer one than any I have ever written, embracing a series of sketches which give the lights and shadows of the "patriarchal institution," written either from observation, incidents which have occurred in the sphere of my personal knowledge, or in the knowledge of my friends. I shall show the *best side* of the thing, and something *faintly approaching the worst*.

Up to this year I have always felt that I had no particular call to meddle with this subject, and I dreaded to expose even my own mind to the full force of its exciting power. But I feel now that the time is come when even a woman or a child who can speak a word for freedom and humanity is bound to speak. The Carthagenian women in the last peril of their state cut off their hair for bow strings to give to the defenders of their country, and such peril and shame as now hangs over this country is worse than Roman slavery, and I hope every woman who can write will not be silent. I have admired and sympathized with the fearless and free spirit of Grace Greenwood, and her letters have done my heart good.[1] My vocation is simply that of *painter*, and my object will be to hold up in the most lifelike and graphic manner possible slavery, its reverses, changes, and the negro character, which I have had ample opportunities for studying. There is no arguing with *pictures*, and everybody is impressed by them, whether they mean to be or not.

I wrote beforehand because I know that you have much matter to arrange, and thought it might not be amiss to give you a hint. The thing may extend through three or four numbers. It will be ready in two or three weeks.

A week or two ago I sent to Mrs. Bailey a story from one of my friends for her paper,[2] requesting also to have my name put down as a subscriber. I have since heard nothing from it. Should the story not prove suitable to her purposes, she will oblige me by redirecting it to me.

[. . .]

Yours with [sincere] esteem,
H. Stowe

Poems by Frances Harper, from *A Brighter Coming Day: A Frances Ellen Watkins Harper Reader*, edited by Frances Smith Foster (New York, N.Y.: Feminist Press, 1990)

Perhaps the preeminent African American poet of the nineteenth century, Frances Ellen Watkins Harper (1825–1911) also succeeded as an influential orator, temperance worker, and suffrage leader. The following three poems were influenced by Harper's familiarity with, and appreciation of, Stowe's works. Harper's poem "Eliza Harris" (published in *The Liberator* and in *Frederick Douglass's Paper* in both 1853 and 1860) casts into verse Chapter 7 of *Uncle Tom's Cabin*. "Eva's Farewell" (published in *Frederick Douglass's Paper*, March 31, 1854) lyrically imagines Chapter 26, and in "To Mrs. Harriet Beecher Stowe" (published in *Frederick Douglass's Paper* in 1854), Harper expresses gratitude to Stowe for her abolitionist efforts.

---

1 [Hedrick's note.] Journalist Grace Greenwood, an alias for Sara Jane Lippincott.
2 [Hedrick's note.] *The Friend of Youth*, a monthly newspaper edited by Margaret L. Bailey.

Eliza Harris

Like a fawn from the arrow, startled and wild,
A woman swept by us, bearing a child;
In her eye was the night of a settled despair,
And her brow was o'ershaded with anguish and care.
She was nearing the river – in reaching the brink,   5
She heeded no danger, she paused not to think!
For she is a mother – her child is a slave –
And she'll give him his freedom, or find him a grave!
It was a vision to haunt us, that innocent face –
So pale in its aspect, so fair in its grace;   10
As the tramp of the horse and the bay of the hound,
With the fetters that gall, were trailing the ground!
She was nerv'd by despair, and strengthened by woe,
As she leap'd o'er the chasms that yawn'd from below;
Death howl'd in the tempest, and rav'd in the blast,   15
But she heard not the sound till the danger was past.
Oh! how shall I speak of my proud country's shame?
Of the stains on her glory, how give them their name?
How say that her banner in mockery waves –
Her "star spangled banner"[1] – o'er millions of slaves?   20
How say that the lawless may torture and chase
A woman whose crime is the hue of her face?
How the depths of the forest may echo around
With the shrieks of despair, and the bay of the hound?
With her step on the ice, and her arm on her child,   25
The danger was fearful, the pathway was wild;
But, aided by Heaven, she gained a free shore,
Where the friends of humanity open'd their door.
So fragile and lovely, so fearfully pale,
Like a lily that bends to the breath of the gale,   30
Save the heave of her breast, and the sway of her hair,
You'd have thought her a statue of fear and despair.
In agony close to her bosom she press'd
The life of her heart, the child of her breast: –
Oh! love from its tenderness gathering might,   35
Had strengthen'd her soul for the dangers of flight.
But she's free – yes, free from the land where the slave
From the hand of oppression must rest in the grave;
Where bondage and torture, where scourges and chains,
Have plac'd on our banner indelible stains.   40

---

1   A reference to the national anthem of the United States, "The Star-Spangled Banner," written by
Francis Scott Key during the British attack on Baltimore in the War of 1812.

Did a fever e'er burning through bosom and brain,
Send a lava-like flood through every vein,
Till it suddenly cooled 'neath a healing spell,
And you knew, oh! the joy! you knew you were well?
So felt this young mother, as a sense of the rest   45
Stole gently and sweetly o'er *her* weary breast,
As her boy looked up, and, wondering, smiled
On the mother whose love had freed her child.
The bloodhounds have miss'd the scent of her way;
The hunter is rifled and foil'd of his prey;   50
Fierce jargon and cursing, with clanking of chains,
Make sounds of strange discord on Liberty's plains.
With the rapture love and fulness of bliss,
She plac'd on his brow a mother's fond kiss: –
Oh! poverty, danger and death she can brave,   55
For the child of her love is no longer a slave!

Eva's Farewell

Farewell, father! I am dying,
    Going to the "glory land,"[1]
Where the sun is ever shining,
    And the zephyr's[2] ever bland.
Where the living fountains flowing,   5
    Quench the pining spirit's thirst;
Where the tree of life is growing,
    Where the crystal fountains burst.
Father! hear that music holy
    Floating from the spirit land!   10
At the pearly gates of glory,
    Radiant angels waiting stand.
Father! kiss your dearest Eva,
    Press her cold and clammy hand,
Ere the glittering hosts receive her,   15
    Welcome to their cherub band.

To Mrs. Harriet Beecher Stowe

I thank thee for thy pleading
    For the helpless of our race

---

1   A reference to heaven as well as to a popular Negro spiritual.
2   The west wind.

Long as our hearts are beating
  In them thou hast a place.
I thank thee for thy pleading   5
  For the fetter'd[1] and the dumb
The blessing of the perishing
  Around thy path shall come.
I thank thee for the kindly words
  That grac'd thy pen of fire,   10
And thrilled upon the living chords
  Of many a heart's deep lyre.[2]
For the sisters of our race
  Thou'st nobly done thy part
Thou hast won thy self a place   15
  In every human heart.
The halo that surrounds thy name
  Hath reached from shore to shore
But thy best and brightest fame
  Is the blessing of the poor.   20

Harriet Beecher Stowe, "Preface" to *A Key to Uncle Tom's Cabin* (1853)

Because many readers doubted the plausibility of her characters, Stowe wrote *A Key to Uncle Tom's Cabin* to provide evidence of the truth behind her fiction. Here in the preface, she urges all Christian readers to examine the evidence of slavery and pray for its abolition.

The work which the writer here presents to the public is one which has been written with no pleasure, and with much pain.

In fictitious writing, it is possible to find refuge from the hard and the terrible, by inventing scenes and characters of a more pleasing nature. No such resource is open in a work of fact; and the subject of this work is one on which the truth, if told at all, must needs be very dreadful. There is no bright side to slavery, as such. Those scenes which are made bright by the generosity and kindness of masters and mistresses, would be brighter still if the element of slavery were withdrawn. There is nothing picturesque or beautiful, in the family attachment of old servants, which is not to be found in countries where these servants are legally free. The tenants on an English estate are often more fond and faithful than if they were slaves. Slavery, therefore, is not the element which forms the picturesque and beautiful of Southern life. What is peculiar to slavery, and distinguishes it from free servitude, is evil, and only evil, and that continually.

---

1   Shackled, chained.
2   Stringed instrument related to a harp; symbol of lyric poetry.

In preparing this work, it has grown much beyond the author's original design. It has so far overrun its limits that she has been obliged to omit one whole department; – that of the characteristics and developments of the colored race in various countries and circumstances. This is more properly the subject for a volume; and she hopes that such an one will soon be prepared by a friend to whom she has transferred her materials.

The author desires to express her thanks particularly to those legal gentlemen who have given her their assistance and support in the legal part of the discussion. She also desires to thank those, at the North and at the South, who have kindly furnished materials for her use. Many more have been supplied than could possibly be used. The book is actually selected out of a mountain of materials.

The great object of the author in writing has been to bring this subject of slavery, as a moral and religious question, before the minds of all those who profess to be followers of Christ, in this country. A minute history has been given of the action of the various denominations on this subject.

The writer has aimed, as far as possible, to say what is true, and only that, without regard to the effect which it may have upon any person or party. She hopes that what she has said will be examined without bitterness, – in that serious and earnest spirit which is appropriate for the examination of so very serious a subject. It would be vain for her to indulge the hope of being wholly free from error. In the wide field which she has been called to go over, there is a possibility of many mistakes. She can only say that she has used the most honest and earnest endeavors to learn the truth.

The book is commended to the candid attention and earnest prayers of all true Christians, throughout the world. May they unite their prayers that Christendom may be delivered from so great an evil as slavery!

Harriet Beecher Stowe, "Uncle Tom" from *A Key to Uncle Tom's Cabin* (1853)

Although the derogatory term "an Uncle Tom" unflatteringly has come to refer to a black person overly servile or deferential to a white person, Stowe insisted that the essence of Uncle Tom existed in actual slaves. Here she relates an acquaintance's account, as well as the story of Josiah Henson, on whom she based the character of Uncle Tom.

The character of Uncle Tom has been objected to as improbable; and yet the writer has received more confirmations of that character, and from a greater variety of sources, than of any other in the book.

Many people have said to her, "I knew an Uncle Tom in such and such a Southern State." All the histories of this kind which have thus been related to her would of themselves, if collected, make a small volume. [. . .]

A last instance parallel with that of Uncle Tom is to be found in the published memoirs of the venerable Josiah Henson, now, as we have said, a clergyman in

Canada. He was "raised" in the State of Maryland. His first recollections were of seeing his father mutilated and covered with blood, suffering the penalty of the law for the crime of raising his hand against a white man, – that white man being the overseer, who had attempted a brutal assault upon his mother. [. . .] Henson grew up in a state of heathenism, without any religious instruction, till, in a camp-meeting, he first heard of Jesus Christ. [. . .] Henson forthwith not only became a Christian, but began to declare the news to those about him [. . .] and though he could not read a word of the Bible or hymn-book, his labors in this line were much prospered. He became immediately a very valuable slave to his master. [. . .] When his [master's] affairs became embarrassed, he formed the design of removing all his negroes into Kentucky, and intrusted the operation entirely to his overseer. Henson was to take them alone, without any other attendant, from Maryland to Kentucky, a distance of some thousands of miles,[1] giving only his promise as a Christian that he would faithfully perform this undertaking. On the way thither they passed through a portion of Ohio, and there Henson was informed that he could now secure his own freedom and that of all his fellows, and he was strongly urged to do it. He was exceedingly tempted and tried, but his Christian principle was invulnerable. No inducements could lead him to feel that it was right for a Christian to violate a pledge solemnly given, and his influence over the whole band was so great that he took them all with him into Kentucky. [. . .] Subsequently to this, his master, in a relenting moment, was induced by a friend to sell him his freedom for four hundred dollars; but, when the excitement of the importunity had passed off, he regretted that he had suffered so valuable a piece of property to leave his hands for so slight a remuneration. By an unworthy artifice, therefore, he got possession of his servant's free papers, and condemned him still to hopeless slavery. [. . .] All the depths of the negro's soul were torn up and thrown into convulsion by this horrible piece of ingratitude, cruelty, and injustice. [. . .] Subsequently to this, his young master was taken violently down with the river fever,[2] and became as helpless as a child. [. . .] The young master was borne in the arms of his faithful servant to the steamboat, and there nursed by him with unremitting attention during the journey up the river; nor did he leave him till he had placed him in his father's arms.

---

1   The distance between Maryland and Kentucky is actually around 200 miles. The states of Virginia and what is now West Virginia lie in between.
2   Probably malaria, a disease transmitted by mosquitoes.

2

Interpretations

2

interpretations

Critical History

Uncle Tom's Cabin first appeared from June 5, 1851 through April 1, 1852 as a series of weekly installments in a Washington, D.C.-based abolitionist journal called the *National Era*. Since the *National Era* was a small publication, the serialized novel did not attract a wide audience. However, when the Boston publisher John P. Jewett acquired the rights to the book and published it as a two-volume set on March 20, 1852, American literary history changed. The first run of 5000 copies sold out in two days, and 50,000 copies were sold in the next eight weeks. Jewett had to run several presses day and night to keep up with the public's demand for the novel. Within the first year, over a million and a half copies were in print.

While sales figures of *Uncle Tom's Cabin* were extraordinary in the United States, they were even stronger in Britain: one and a half million copies of the travails of Eliza, Eva, and Uncle Tom were sold to British readers in the first year. As Stowe biographer Joan Hedrick notes, the "British saw that the originality of the book sprang from Stowe's grasp of the nationality of her material: an epic theme – republican ideals in conflict with a feudal institution – was enshrined in a narrative bristling with regional types. [. . .] At the same time, the resonances between race and class operated powerfully on British readers to tap a sympathy with the poor and oppressed."[1] George Cruikshank, who earned acclaim as the illustrator of Charles Dickens's novels, did the engravings for the first British edition of *Uncle Tom's Cabin*.

Abolition was not a nationally popular cause in the United States at mid-century: since abolitionists dared to challenge national policy validating slavery, they were widely considered dangerous, immoral, and impolite trouble-makers. By publicly aligning herself, a proper Christian woman from a socially prominent family, with law breakers who claimed a superior moral position, Stowe took a great risk, and thus the success of her book is even more astounding. Furthermore, Stowe featured pioneering depictions of slave owners as not all

1   Joan Hedrick, *Harriet Beecher Stowe: A Life* (New York, N.Y.: Oxford University Press, 1994), 234.

bad; in fact, she portrays slave owners as just as vexed and multifaceted as slaves and abolitionists.

From 1852 to 1861 at least twenty-seven pro-slavery works were published by authors who wanted to counteract Stowe's attack on slavery. These works featured benevolent slave masters and satisfied slaves, and formed a body of anti-Uncle Tom literature.

The section on Early Critical Reception selects several contemporary book reviews that give an idea of the range of early responses to *Uncle Tom's Cabin*. For example, the laudatory reviews by Charles Briggs, Charles Dickens, the Boston *Morning Post*, and William Lloyd Garrison suggest the triumph and significance of the novel. However, the reviewer for the *Southern Literary Messenger* abhors the novel, condemning it as a collection of lies intended to give readers an intentionally false and negative perception of slavery.

Reviews and secondary materials on *Uncle Tom's Cabin* are voluminous: the pieces excerpted here represent only a small taste of the numerous reactions generated by Stowe's highly polemical novel. The twentieth-century criticism selected for the Sourcebook can be organized into roughly three perspectives: abolition and race, domesticity and women's tradition, and Christian charity.

While readers can fairly safely agree that Stowe intended her novel to arouse sympathy against slavery and in favor of abolition, they sometimes heatedly disagree on the efficacy of methods and literary techniques Stowe employed. For example, while some readers may laud Stowe's acknowledgment of slaves' personhood, others decry as racist her stereotyping of African Americans. While some readers salute Stowe's efforts to help emancipation, others fault her for showing too much support for colonization, which meant encouraging newly liberated African Americans to go to Africa rather than remain free and equal in the United States.

James Baldwin's essay "Everybody's Protest Novel", perhaps most famously, takes Stowe to task for perpetuating racist stereotypes. Such other critics as Susan Gillman, Jim O'Loughlin, Arthur Riss, Peter Stonely, and Cynthia Griffin Wolff articulate various responses to the novel that interrogate issues of race and abolition.

Although issues of race certainly figure prominently in any discussion of *Uncle Tom's Cabin*, Stowe's conception of the power of domesticity and the sentimental tradition also strongly infuses her novel and attendant critical attention. As Jane Tompkins argues, *Uncle Tom's Cabin* "retells the culture's central religious myth – the story of the crucifixion – in terms of the nation's greatest political conflict – slavery – and of its most cherished social beliefs – the sanctity of motherhood and the family" (**p. 46**). By linking the saving power of love, the holiness of selfless motherhood, and the belief in a merciful God, Stowe casts slavery as a direct assault on all that society holds dear. According to her son, Stowe said about *Uncle Tom's Cabin* that "[t]his story is to show how Jesus Christ, who liveth and was dead, and now is alive and forevermore, has still a mother's love for the poor and lowly."[2]

---

2   Charles Edward Stowe, *Life of Harriet Beecher Stowe Compiled from Her Letters and Journals* (Boston, Mass.: Houghton Mifflin, 1890), 154.

Many American novels written by women in the nineteenth century have been labeled as sentimental, a term which in general designates a style noted for its emphasis on excessive emotion, highly wrought scenes, didacticism, and an abundance of tears, no matter what the content or subject of the novel itself, while almost no male writers' novels have been labeled as such. Labeling women's novels as sentimental usually means that the work is not as serious, philosophical, or intellectually engaged as men's writing. Tompkins and other critics, however, have argued the opposite: that the nineteenth-century popular, sentimental, domestic women's novel "represents a monumental effort to reorganize culture from the women's point of view; that this body of work is remarkable for its intellectual complexity, ambition, and resourcefulness; and that, in certain cases, it offers a critique of American society far more devastating than any delivered by better-known critics such as Hawthorne and Melville" (**p. 43**). Excerpts from essays by Tompkins, as well as from essays by Gillian Brown and Marianne Noble, explore *Uncle Tom's Cabin* from positions informed by feminist scholarship.

Uncle Tom's Cabin is a very Christian novel – it begins by invoking an "enlightened and Christianized community" (**p. 83**), refers to Christian belief and action throughout, and concludes with a mighty ending intoning that both "North and South have been guilty before God; and the *Christian church* has a heavy account to answer" and calling for "repentance, justice and mercy" (**p. 151**). Therefore, it is not surprising that many critics have been interested in looking at the religious aspects and implications of the novel. Excerpts from essays by Lawrence Buell, Amy Schrager Lang, and Jean Fagan Yellin illustrate the interest critics take in Stowe's literary religious vision.

All of these pieces of modern criticism demonstrate the consistent interest in and relevance of *Uncle Tom's Cabin* for readers in the twenty-first century. The novel still asks us to consider salient questions of representation: does representation of race or racism destroy or reinforce stereotypes? Does representation of domesticity validate women's work or consign it to an unequal sphere? Does the use of sentiment positively or negatively affect representation? Does the novel stand as a significant literary achievement or a rehashing of sentimental convention? The fact that readers still wrestle with these questions indicates that the novel still speaks to us more than a century and a half after its first appearance.

Finally, in this Section, the Sourcebook will examine a different type of interpretation of the novel – the work in performance. Stage versions of *Uncle Tom's Cabin*, wildly popular in the years following publication of the novel, presented Uncle Tom, intended by Stowe to be a noble hero, as a bumbling, subservient fool who bows down to the white man. The insult, "an Uncle Tom," derives from staged performances of the novel over which Stowe had no control.

Early Critical Reception

From **Charles F. Briggs, "Uncle Tomitudes,"** *Putnam's Monthly Magazine* (January 1853): 97–102

Charles F. Briggs (1804–77) was a novelist and editor of several magazines, including *The Broadway Journal*, which he founded in 1854 with Edgar Allan Poe. In calling *Uncle Tom's Cabin* a "live book," Briggs praises the immediate sense of deep feeling one experiences when reading the novel. Briggs favourably compares Stowe's work to that of Washington Irving, Nathaniel Hawthorne, Herman Melville, and James Fenimore Cooper: while Stowe's novel does not share the "delicacies of language" or the same sweeping depiction of scenery, *Uncle Tom's Cabin* is superior in its "broader, deeper, higher and holier sympathies," and its "finer delineations of character, a wider scope of observation, a more purely American spirit, and a more vigorous narrative faculty."

[The success achieved by *Uncle Tom's Cabin*] does not, by any means, argue that [it] is superior to all other books: but it is an unmistakable indication that it is a live book, and that it will continue to live when many other books which have been pronounced immortal, shall be dead and buried in an oblivion, from which there is no resurrection.

Uncle Tom is not only a miracle of itself, but it announces the commencement of a miraculous Era in the literary world.

Not the least remarkable among the phenomena that have attended the publication of *Uncle Tom* has been the numerous works written expressly to counteract the impressions which the book was supposed likely to make. This is something entirely new in literature. It is one of the most striking testimonials to the intrinsic merit of the work that it should be thought necessary to neutralize its influence by issuing other romances to prove that *Uncle Tom* is a fiction. Nothing of the kind was ever before deemed necessary. [. . .] *Uncle Tom* had scarcely seen the light when dozens of steel pens were set at work to prove him an impostor, and his author an ignoramus [. . .]

[*Uncle Tom's Cabin*] is a live book, and it talks to its readers as if it were alive. It first awakens their attention, arrests their thoughts, touches their sympathies, rouses their curiosity, and creates such an interest in the story it is telling, that they cannot let it drop until the whole story is told. And this is done, not because it is a tale of slavery, but in spite of it. [. . .] It is the consummate art of the story teller that has given popularity to *Uncle Tom's Cabin*, and nothing else. [. . .]

There are not, in *Uncle Tom's Cabin*, any of the delicacies of language which impart so great a charm to the writings of Irving and Hawthorne, nor any descriptions of scenery such as abound in the romances of Cooper,[1] nor any thing like the bewildering sensuousness of *Typee* by Melville; but there are broader, deeper, higher and holier sympathies than can be found in our other romances; finer delineations of character, a wider scope of observation, a more purely American spirit, and a more vigorous narrative faculty. We can name no novel, after [Fielding's] *Tom Jones*, that is superior to *Uncle Tom* in constructive ability. The interest of the narrative begins in the first page and is continued with consummate skill to the last. [. . .]

In no other American book that we have read, are there so many well-delineated American characters; the greater part of them are wholly new in fiction. [. . .] Mrs. Stowe's book gives a much more agreeable picture of Southern slavery than any of the works we have seen which profess to give the right side of the tapestry. A desire to degrade America surely cannot be the reason why the representation of dramatic scenes in *Uncle Tom* have proved so attractive in our own theatres.[2]

Charles Dickens, letter of July 17, 1852

In this personal letter to Stowe, the great British novelist Charles Dickens (1812–70) expresses his simultaneous admiration of, and hesitation about, *Uncle Tom's Cabin*.

I have read [*Uncle Tom's Cabin*] with the deepest interest and sympathy, and admire, more than I can express to you, both the generous feeling which inspired it, and the admirable power with which it is executed.

If I might suggest a fault in what has so charmed me, it would be that you go too far and seek to prove too much. The wrongs and atrocities of slavery are, God knows! case enough. I doubt there being any warrant for making out the African race to be a great race, or for supposing the future destinies of the world to lie in that direction: and I think this extreme championship likely to repel some useful sympathy and support.

---

1 Novelist James Fenimore Cooper (1789–1851) was famous for his idealization of the American landscape and the Indians in such works as *The Last of the Mohicans* (1826) and *The Deerslayer* (1841).
2 For a discussion of theatrical adaptations of *Uncle Tom's Cabin* see **pp. 75–7**.

Your book is worthy of any head and any heart that ever inspired a book. I am much your debtor, and I thank you most fervently and sincerely.

Anonymous, review of *Uncle Tom's Cabin*, Boston *Morning Post*, 1852

In this laudatory review, the writer praises Stowe for the brilliance of her work and for her ability to present both sides of an issue, a skill the review equates with "masculine" genius.

Since *Jane Eyre* [1847], no book has had so sudden and so great a success on this side of the Atlantic as *Uncle Tom's Cabin*. Everybody has read it, is reading it, or is about to read it. And certainly it is one of the most remarkable literary productions of the time – an evident result of some of the highest attributes of the novel writer. [. . .]

Uncle Tom's Cabin, as much as any novel we know of, is stamped on every page with genius. The author cannot touch a single incident without showing that she bears the sacred fire. [. . .] Not one word in the book suggests mediocrity, whether the pictures of slavery please or displease. And the death of Eva! We have said that some chapters are beyond criticism – the reader will find them so. And with all the pathos and intensity of most of the story, there is no jot of dullness – no harping on one string. A vein of humor and drollery meanders through it, and one is often laughing with wet eyes.

But brilliant as is *Uncle Tom's Cabin* as a literary work, it is yet more creditable to the author in another point of view. It proves that unlike most women, and very many men, Mrs. Stowe has the ability of looking on both sides of one question. [. . .] The entire fiction is filled with instances of this peculiar power of the author to look on both sides of a question at once, and this (so called) masculine quality of mind is sustained by an exceeding ease in the management of details and the handling of masculine facts of all sorts. One wonders, indeed, where a lady could pick up so much stuff, and how she could acquire such free and easy manners in disposing of it. Everything is fish that comes to her net, and she is equally at home with saint or sinner, black or white, high or low. She never suffers any mock-modesty, reverence or respect for any world-prejudice whatever to stand in the way of truth of portraiture or naturalness of dialogue.

Anonymous, review of *Uncle Tom's Cabin*, *Liberator*, March 26, 1852

Abolitionist William Lloyd Garrison's newspaper, the *Liberator*, published in Boston, was perhaps the most important antislavery newspaper. It published important news pieces, essays, and opinions about slavery and its ills. This positive review of *Uncle Tom's Cabin* lent Stowe's antislavery message an air of credibility.

[. . .] In the execution of her very difficult task, Mrs. Stowe has displayed rare descriptive powers, a familiar acquaintance with slavery under its best and worst phases, uncommon moral and philosophical acumen, great facility of thought and expression, feelings and emotions of the strongest character. Intimate as we have been, for a score of years, with the features and operations of the slave system, and often as we have listened to the recitals of its horrors from the lips of the poor hunted fugitives, we confess to the frequent moistening of our eyes, and the making of our heart grow liquid as water, and the trembling of every nerve within us, in the perusal of the incidents and scenes so vividly depicted in her pages. [. . .]

[Uncle Tom's] character is sketched with great power and rare religious perception. It triumphantly exemplifies the nature, tendency and results of CHRISTIAN NON-RESISTANCE. We are curious to know whether Mrs. Stowe is a believer in the duty of non-resistance for the white man, under all possible outrage and peril, as well as for the black man; whether she is for self-defense on her own part, or that of her husband or friends or country, in case of malignant assault, or whether she impartially disarms all mankind in the name of Christ, be the danger or suffering what it may. [. . .]

Talk not of overcoming evil with good – it is madness! Talk not of peacefully submitting to chains and stripes – it is base servility! Talk not of servants being obedient to their masters – let the blood of tyrants flow! How is this to be explained or reconciled? Is there one law of submission and non-resistance for the black man, and another law of rebellion and conflict for the white man? When it is the whites who are trodden in the dust, does Christ justify them in taking up arms to vindicate their rights? And when it is the blacks who are thus treated, does Christ require them to be patient, harmless, long-suffering, and forgiving? And are there two Christs?

Anonymous, review of *Uncle Tom's Cabin*, *Southern Literary Messenger,* 1853

In the pro-slavery South, *Uncle Tom's Cabin* inflamed many readers' anger. In this review, the writer takes the term "fiction" to task, using the genre to condemn the novel as nothing but falsehood.

[*Uncle Tom's Cabin*] is a fiction – professedly a fiction; but, unlike other works of the same type, its purpose is not amusement, but proselytism.

We have examined the production of Mrs. Harriet Beecher Stowe, which we purpose to review, and we discover it to belong to [this] class, and to be one of the most reprehensible specimens of the tribe. [. . .] It is a fiction throughout; a fiction in form; a fiction in its facts; a fiction in its representations and coloring; a fiction in its statements; a fiction in its sentiments, a fiction in its morals, a fiction in its religion; a fiction in its inferences; a fiction equally with regard to the subjects it is designed to expound, and with respect to the manner of their exposition. It is a fiction, not for the sake of more effectually communicating truth; but for the purpose of more effectually disseminating a slander. It is a fictitious or fanciful representation for the sake of producing fictitious or false impressions. Fiction is its form and falsehood is its end.

From **Marva Banks, "*Uncle Tom's Cabin* and the Antebellum Black Response,"** in *Readers in History: Nineteenth-Century American Literature and the Contexts of Response*, ed. James L. Machor (Baltimore, Md.: Johns Hopkins University Press, 1993)

Although this extract is taken from a recently published work, it offers great insight on the early critical reception of the novel by black readers. For that reason, it is included here, rather than in the following section alongside other modern critical works.

As Marva Banks's careful research shows, antebellum black readers of *Uncle Tom's Cabin* held widely varying views of the novel. Many African Americans, including Frederick Douglass, eagerly anticipated a novel that would serve the abolitionist cause. But many black readers deplored Stowe's perpetuation of images of black passivity and inferiority, images that could be used to justify continued slavery. The final chapter of the novel, "Concluding Remarks," presented particularly difficult problems for the antebellum black reader, as Banks explains.

[. . .] When Stowe's novel appeared in book form in March 1852, the responses of white readers in Europe and the United States – North and South – were carefully recorded and commented upon. These comments became part of a substantial history of reader response. However, this rather extensive history has virtually ignored black readers' responses to *Uncle Tom's Cabin*. It is as if the black reader did not exist or was a mere phantom who could say with Ralph Ellison's protagonist, "I am invisible, understand, simply because people refuse to see me." Though ignored historically, however, the antebellum black audience did exist and had opinions regarding Stowe and her novel. Between 1852, when *Uncle Tom's Cabin* was published in book form, and 1855, when comments about the novel began to diminish, over two hundred articles containing comments by black readers appeared in the antebellum black press. Seven black papers regularly printed these comments. Of the seven, *Frederick Douglass' Paper*[1] carried most of these responses.

[. . .] The purpose of this essay is to analyze surviving black responses to Stowe's novel, recorded in the antebellum black press, as products of the specific historical conditions blacks faced in America between 1852 and 1855, and to show how those responses embody an awareness among black readers of the connections between Stowe's novel and their peculiar historical moment. [. . .]

As an avenue into the particular character of the mid-nineteenth-century black

---

1   Abolitionist newspaper published by Douglass from 1851 to 1860.

responses to *Uncle Tom's Cabin*, I want to turn briefly to James Baldwin's 1949 essay "Everybody's Protest Novel," [**see pp. 40–2**] which, I would argue, provides retroactively a kind of preparatory gloss on the responses by blacks almost a hundred year earlier. Epitomizing the reactions of twentieth-century black critics to Stowe's novel, Baldwin [. . .] attacks most forcefully Stowe's denial of the individual humanity of blacks, as evidenced by her reducing all of her black characters to "stock" personalities. "Apart from her [. . .] procession of field hand [and] house niggers," notes Baldwin, "she has only three other Negroes, only one of which is truly Negroid." For Baldwin, the mixture of these stereotypes with Stowe's "self-righteous, virtuous sentimentalizing" creates a dangerous element in the novel. [. . .] What is significant here is that all four of the concerns found in some degree in Baldwin's essay also characterize antebellum black responses: (1) *Uncle Tom's Cabin* as antislavery propaganda, (2) *Uncle Tom's Cabin* as promulgator of colonizationist ideas, (3) *Uncle Tom's Cabin* as a catalogue of sentimental racism, and (4) Stowe's personality as confirmation of blacks' generally ambivalent opinions of the novel. But whereas Baldwin emphasizes the novel's racist stereotyping and treats only obliquely the issue of colonization, it was the latter that eventually constituted the major focus through which antebellum blacks responded to *Uncle Tom's Cabin*. [. . .]

The initial perception blacks had of *Uncle Tom's Cabin* was that it served as an important antislavery weapon. And indeed it was a powerful argument against it. Naturally, the early black reaction to Stowe's novel was enthusiastic. In fact, as early as April 8, 1852, less than a month after the book's publication, Frederick Douglass eagerly announced in his *Paper* that "Uncle Tom's Cabin, the thrilling story from the pen of Mrs. Stowe would soon be on sale."[2] [. . .]

Although many blacks were understandably excited by the astounding antislavery power of Stowe's novel, as evidenced by the number of changed opinions regarding slavery, they soon discovered that *Uncle Tom's Cabin* possessed an equivalent capacity to promulgate certain racist images. [. . .] Indeed, Stowe's sympathy for African colonization and her proclivity to racial stereotypes reinforced, in important ways, the dominant argument of proslavery advocates: white supremacy.

The African colonization scheme posed a real danger to free blacks. Proof of that danger is the fact that approximately 30,000 blacks had been deported involuntarily since the founding of the American Colonization Society in 1816. [. . .] During the 1850s Frederick Douglass led the attack against African emigration. The columns of his *Paper* were dominated by the numerous discussions opposing the emigration of black Americans. [. . .]

The African colonization threat reached a new intensity in 1852 when the book version of *Uncle Tom's Cabin* appeared and was interpreted as showing Stowe's favorable opinion toward colonization. To be sure, the novel presents at least two dramatic expressions of procolonization sympathy. We see the first example when George Harris, despairing of ever achieving success in America or in Canada,

---

2   [Banks's note.] "Uncle Tom's Cabin," *Frederick Douglass' Paper* (April 8, 1852): 2.

seeks an alternative homeland. Where will he go, he wonders. The answer is Africa. [. . .] "I want a country, a nation of my own," Harris says. "I think the African race has peculiarities, yet to be unfolded in light of civilization and Christianity". Although Harris recognizes the sinister machinations impelling white support of colonization, he cannot overlook the opportunity Liberia[3] offers blacks to build their own independent nation. Thus determined to establish his own nation, George Harris departs with his family for Africa.

The second example – and the one that antebellum blacks focused on as the more telling index to the novel's and Stowe's personal views on the expatriation of blacks to Africa – appears in the chapter entitled "Concluding Remarks." Having disposed of her major black characters in Africa, Stowe presents her solution to the problem of what to do with free blacks in nineteenth-century America. [. . .] Stowe recommends emigration for blacks and gives explicit instructions as to how blacks should be prepared for their exportation to Africa [. . .]

Although the majority of Stowe's black characters accept her remedy for the race problem and depart for Liberia, black abolitionists were not so easily persuaded that her call for African emigration was for them an acceptable solution. At the annual meeting of the American and Foreign Anti-Slavery Society in Rochester, New York, on May 11, 1852, fugitive slave and prominent abolitionist George T. Downing led the black delegates in condemning the chapter of *Uncle Tom's Cabin* that dealt favorably with colonization. [. . .]

Just as troubling for many blacks was Stowe's use of racial stereotypes. For in *Uncle Tom's Cabin* she dramatizes the prevailing notion of black subjugation through her depiction of blacks as naturally obedient, Christian, childlike, and forgiving. And while these qualities are found in many of Stowe's blacks [. . .] and are not limited to Tom, it is the latter's characterization that most offended blacks. [. . .]

Tom's Christian piety caused antebellum blacks much consternation [. . .] [A] correspondent of the *Provincial Freeman* for July 22, 1854, took perhaps the strongest stand by declaring that "Uncle Tom must be killed" – in other words, the image of black subservience that Tom's character engendered must be discouraged, done away with. Because the submissive, docile quality embodied by Tom was perceived by many blacks to be subversive to black progress, the spirit and the image would have to be "killed." For many black readers of the novel, the character of Tom was a telling sign that Stowe's racism lined up perfectly with the general sentiment of mainstream nineteenth-century America.

What blacks suspected as racial ambivalence in Stowe's novel was confirmed for them in her personality, particularly in her personal response to blacks. Although she had come in contact with a number of blacks in her hometown of Litchfield, Connecticut, in Cincinnati, Ohio, and during her brief tour of a Kentucky slave plantation, and though she was often patronizing and benevolent

---

3   The American Colonization Society was founded in 1817 with the goal to resettle freed blacks in the African country of Liberia.

toward blacks, Stowe felt they occupied a subservient position to whites as chattel and wage slaves.[4] In this regard, she was like Ophelia in *Uncle Tom's Cabin*: she detested slavery, but could not accept blacks as her equal. Stowe was never as committed an abolitionist as were her contemporaries Lucretia Mott, Lydia Child, or the Grimke sisters.[5] She remained on the periphery of abolitionism. [. . .] Apparently she sincerely felt that blacks could develop their potential more fully in Africa than in the United States. [. . .] Stowe's behavior clearly embodied a mixture of abolition sentiment and racist doctrine – a combination which helped to prohibit the fulfillment of liberty and equality for nineteenth-century blacks.

The key to understanding the complex nature of the racial ambivalence in Stowe's novel and in her personality, and the particular responses blacks made to the novel, lies in the historical moment that inspired the novel and these reactions. For Stowe was as much influenced by her race, moment, and milieu when she created *Uncle Tom's Cabin* as the black readers who responded to it were affected by theirs. Black responses to *Uncle Tom's Cabin* were like Stowe's view on race – ambivalent. Initially, blacks eagerly heralded it and were optimistic about the impetus it would give to the abolitionist cause. But as blacks became increasingly aware that Stowe's novel had an equivalent power to foster certain images of black inferiority and could therefore be used to bolster the proslavery argument, their early enthusiasm often changed to skepticism and then to anger. Understandably, black responses changed with black perceptions of the complex dynamics of the novel and the power it had to increase or to retard freedom and equality for blacks. Thus, what initially appeared as a blessing to convert the hearts of the nation to abolitionism became for black readers, responding to *Uncle Tom's Cabin* in the context of racist and pro-colonization ideology at mid-century, a curse that encouraged continuation of the doctrine of white supremacy in America.

---

4 [Banks's note.] John R. Adams, *Harriet Beecher Stowe* (New York, N.Y.: Twayne, 1963), 52.
5 Lucretia Mott (1793–1880) was a feminist, abolitionist, Quaker minister, and advocate of social justice. Lydia Maria Child (1802–80) gained prominence as a novelist, editor, short fiction writer, and abolitionist. Sisters Sarah Moore Grimke (1792–1873) and Angelina Grimke (1805–79) were leading lecturers, abolitionists, feminist activists, and authors.

Modern Criticism

From **James Baldwin, "Everybody's Protest Novel,"** in *Notes of a Native Son* (New York, N.Y.: Dial Press, 1949)

Perhaps the best known essay that attacks *Uncle Tom's Cabin*, Baldwin's "Everybody's Protest Novel" first appeared in a collection of Baldwin's essays in 1949. Baldwin, a major African American novelist who wrote such masterpieces as *Go Tell It on the Mountain* (1953), *Another Country* (1962), and *Notes of a Native Son* (1955), as well as the much-anthologized short story "Sonny's Blues" (1957), deplores Stowe's use of sentiment and her dehumanizing lack of "true" black characters. These narrative faults, he contends, undermine Stowe's social protest intentions. Baldwin's views speak for many twentieth-century black critics of Stowe's novel and reflect numerous nineteenth-century voices as well, as Marva Banks points out in her essay, "*Uncle Tom's Cabin* and the Antebellum Black Response" (**pp. 36–9**).

[. . .] *Uncle Tom's Cabin* is a very bad novel, having, in its self-righteous, virtuous sentimentality, much in common with *Little Women*.[1] Sentimentality, the ostentatious parading of excessive and spurious emotion, is the mark of dishonesty, the inability to feel; the wet eyes of the sentimentalist betray his aversion to experience, his fear of life, his arid heart; and it is always, therefore, the signal of secret and violent inhumanity, the mask of cruelty. *Uncle Tom's Cabin* – like its multitudinous, hard-boiled descendants – is a catalogue of violence. This is explained by the nature of Mrs. Stowe's subject matter, her laudable determination to flinch from nothing in presenting the complete picture; an explanation which falters only if we pause to ask whether or not her picture is indeed complete; and what constriction or failure of perception forced her to so depend on the description of brutality – unmotivated, senseless – and to leave unanswered and unnoticed the

---

1 Famous girls' novel published in 1868 by Louisa May Alcott (1832–88).

only important question: what it was, after all, that moved her people to such deeds.

But this, let us say, was beyond Mrs. Stowe's powers; she was not so much a novelist as an impassioned pamphleteer; her book was not intended to do anything more than prove that slavery was wrong; was, in fact, perfectly horrible. This makes material for a pamphlet but it is hardly enough for a novel [. . .]

Apart from her lively procession of field hands, house niggers, Chloe, Topsy, etc. – who are the stock, lovable figures presenting no problem – she has only three other Negroes in the book. These are the important ones and two of them may be dismissed immediately, since we have only the author's word that they are Negro and they are, in all other respects, as white as she can make them. The two are George and Eliza, a married couple with a wholly adorable child – whose quaintness, incidentally, and whose charm, rather put one in mind of a darky bootblack doing a buck and wing to the clatter of condescending coins. Eliza is a beautiful, pious hybrid, light enough to pass – the heroine of *Quality* might, indeed, be her reincarnation – differing from the genteel mistress who has overseered her education only in the respect that she is a servant. George is darker, but makes up for it by being a mechanical genius, and is, moreover, sufficiently un-Negroid to pass through town, a fugitive from his master, disguised as a Spanish gentleman, attracting no attention whatever beyond admiration. They are a race apart from Topsy. It transpires by the end of the novel, through one of those energetic, last-minute convolutions of the plot, that Eliza has some connection with French gentility. The figure from whom the novel takes its name, Uncle Tom, who is a figure of controversy yet, is jet-black, wooly-haired, illiterate; and he is phenomenally forbearing. He has to be; he is black; only through this forbearance can he survive or triumph. [. . .] His triumph is metaphysical, unearthly; since he is black, born without the light, it is only through humility, the incessant mortification of the flesh, that he can enter into communion with God or man. The virtuous rage of Mrs. Stowe is motivated by nothing so temporal as a concern for the relationship of men to one another – or, even, as she would have claimed, by a concern for their relationship to God – but merely by a panic of being hurled into the flames, of being caught in traffic with the devil. She embraced this merciless doctrine with all her heart, bargaining shamelessly before the throne of grace: God and salvation becoming her personal property, purchased with the coin of her virtue. Here, black equates with evil and white with grace; if, being mindful of the necessity of good works, she could not cast out the blacks – a wretched, huddled mass,[2] apparently, claiming, like an obsession, her inner eye – she could not embrace them either without purifying them of sin. [. . .] Tom, therefore, her only black man, has been robbed of his humanity and divested of his sex. It is the price for that darkness with which he has been branded.

---

2 A reference to the line "Give me your tired, your poor, / Your huddled masses yearning to breathe free" from Emma Lazarus's 1883 sonnet "The New Colossus," engraved on a tablet on the pedestal of the Statue of Liberty in New York City's harbor, one of the principal points of entry to the United States for new immigrants.

Uncle Tom's Cabin, then, is activated by what might be called a theological terror, the terror of damnation; and the spirit that breathes in this book, hot, self-righteous, fearful, is not different from that spirit of medieval times which sought to exorcize evil by burning witches; and is not different from that terror which activates a lynch mob. [. . .] This, notwithstanding that the avowed aim of the American protest novel is to bring greater freedom to the oppressed. They are forgiven, on the strength of these good intentions, whatever violence they do to language, whatever excessive demands they make of credibility.

From **Jane Tompkins, "Sentimental Power: *Uncle Tom's Cabin* and the Politics of Literary History,"** in *Sensational Designs: The Cultural Work of American Fiction, 1790–1860* (New York, N.Y.: Oxford University Press, 1985)

A landmark piece of criticism, Jane Tompkins's essay on *Uncle Tom's Cabin* changed critical opinion of the novel and opened the door for a new generation of readers and scholars. In this essay, Tompkins argues for the political and social importance of the domestic novel and shows how sentiment, unjustly derided as women's sloppy emotions, can move and change the world. With this argument, Tompkins teaches readers of American literature to rethink the way literary value is assigned.

Once, during a difficult period of my life, I lived in the basement of a house on Forest Street in Hartford, Connecticut, which had belonged to Isabella Beecher Hooker – Harriet Beecher Stowe's half-sister. [. . .] When I lived in that basement, however, I knew nothing of Stowe, or of the Beechers, or of the utopian visions of nineteenth-century American women. I made a reverential visit to the Mark Twain house a few blocks away, took photographs of his study, and completely ignored Stowe's own house – also open to the public – which stood across the lawn. Why should I go? Neither I nor anyone I knew regarded Stowe as a serious writer. At the time, I was giving my first lecture course in the American Renaissance – concentrated exclusively on Hawthorne, Melville, Poe, Emerson, Thoreau, and Whitman – and although *Uncle Tom's Cabin* was written in exactly the same period, and although it is probably the most influential book ever written by an American, I would never have dreamed of including it on my reading list. To begin with, its very popularity would have militated against it [. . .] But despite the influence of the women's movement, despite the explosion of work in nineteenth-century American social history, and despite the new historicism that is infiltrating literary studies, the women, like Stowe, whose names were household words in the nineteenth century – women such as Susan Warner, Sarah J. Hale, Augusta Evans, Elizabeth Stuart Phelps, her daughter Mary, who took the same name, and Frances Hodgson Burnett – these women remain excluded from the literary canon.[1] And while it has recently become fashionable to study their works as examples of cultural deformation, even critics who have invested their professional careers in that study and who declare themselves feminists still refer to their novels as trash.

My principal target of concern, however, is not feminists who have written on popular women novelists of the nineteenth century, but the male-dominated scholarly tradition that controls both the canon of American literature (from which these novelists are excluded) and the critical perspective that interprets the canon for society. [. . .] The very grounds on which sentimental fiction has been dismissed by its detractors, grounds which have come to seem universal standards of aesthetic judgment, were established in a struggle to supplant the tradition of evangelical piety and moral commitment these novelists represent. In reaction against their world view, and perhaps even more against their success, twentieth-century critics have taught generations of students to equate popularity with debasement, emotionality with ineffectiveness, religiosity with fakery, domesticity with triviality, and all of these, implicitly, with womanly inferiority.

In this view, sentimental novels written by women in the nineteenth century were responsible for a series of cultural evils whose effects still plague us: the degeneration of American religion from theological rigor to anti-intellectual consumerism, the rationalization of an unjust economic order, the propagation of the debased images of modern mass culture, and the encouragement of self-indulgence and narcissism in literature's most avid readers – women. [. . .] In contrast to male authors such as Thoreau, Whitman, and Melville, who are celebrated as models of intellectual daring and honesty, these women are generally thought to have traded in false stereotypes, dishing out weak-minded pap to nourish the prejudices of an ill-educated and underemployed female readership. Self-deluded and unable to face the harsh facts of a competitive society, they are portrayed as manipulators of a gullible public who kept their readers imprisoned in a dream world of self-justifying clichés. Their fight against the evils of their society was a fixed match from the start.

The thesis I will argue in this chapter is diametrically opposed to these portrayals. It holds that the popular domestic novel of the nineteenth century represents a monumental effort to reorganize culture from the woman's point of view; that this body of work is remarkable for its intellectual complexity, ambition, and resourcefulness; and that, in certain cases, it offers a critique of American society far more devastating than any delivered by better-known critics such as Hawthorne and Melville. Finally, it suggests that the enormous popularity of these novels, which has been cause for suspicion bordering on disgust, is a reason for paying close attention to them. *Uncle Tom's Cabin* was, in almost any

---

1 Susan Warner (1819–85) published *The Wide, Wide World* (1851), a novel that sold over a million copies. Sarah Josepha Hale (1788–1879), author and editor, served for forty years as editor of the influential magazine *Godey's Lady's Book*. Augusta Evans (1835–1909) wrote nine novels and numerous pieces of journalism. Elizabeth Stuart Phelps (1815–52) was a novelist, short story writer, and children's author. Her daughter, Elizabeth Stuart Phelps Ward (1844–1911), also known as Mary, as well wrote novels, short stories, essays, children's pieces, and poetry. Frances Hodgson Burnett (1849–1924) wrote over fifty novels and stories for adults and children.

terms one can think of, the most important book of the century. It was the first American novel ever to sell over a million copies and its impact is generally thought to have been incalculable. Expressive of and responsible for the values of its time, it also belongs to a genre, the sentimental novel, whose chief characteristic is that it is written by, for, and about women. In this respect, *Uncle Tom's Cabin* is not exceptional but representative. It is the *summa theologica* of nineteenth-century America's religion of domesticity, a brilliant redaction of the culture's favorite story about itself – the story of salvation through motherly love. Out of the ideological materials at their disposal, the sentimental novelists elaborated a myth that gave women the central position of power and authority in the culture; and of these efforts *Uncle Tom's Cabin* is the most dazzling exemplar.

I have used words like "monumental" and "dazzling" to describe Stowe's novel and the tradition of which it is a part because they have for too long been the casualties of a set of critical attitudes that equate intellectual merit with a certain kind of argumentative discourse and certain kinds of subject matter. A long tradition of academic parochialism has enforced this sort of discourse through a series of cultural contrasts: light "feminine" novels vs. toughminded intellectual treatises; domestic "chattiness" vs. serious thinking; and summarily, the "damned mob of scribbling women" vs. a few giant intellects, unappreciated and misunderstood in their time, struggling manfully against a flood of sentimental rubbish.

The inability of twentieth-century critics either to appreciate the complexity and scope of a novel like Stowe's, or to account for its enormous popular success, stems from their assumptions about the nature and function of literature. In modernist thinking, literature is by definition a form of discourse that has no designs on the world. It does not attempt to change things, but merely to represent them, and it does so in a specifically literary language whose claim to value lies in its uniqueness. Consequently, works whose stated purpose is to influence the course of history, and which therefore employ a language that is not only not unique but common and accessible to everyone, do not qualify as works of art. Literary texts, such as the sentimental novel, that make continual and obvious appeals to the reader's emotions and use technical devices that are distinguished by their utter conventionality, epitomize the opposite of everything that good literature is supposed to be. [. . .]

It is not my purpose, however, to drag Hawthorne and Melville from their pedestals, nor to claim that the novels of Stowe, Fanny Fern,[2] and Elizabeth Stuart Phelps are good in the same way that *Moby-Dick* and *The Scarlet Letter* are; rather, I will argue that the work of the sentimental writers is complex and significant in ways *other than* those that characterize the established masterpieces. I will ask the reader to set aside some familiar categories for evaluating fiction –

---

2   Fanny Fern (the pen name of Sarah Willis Parton, 1811–72), known for her wit, humor, and bold feminist agenda, was a journalist, novelist (most celebrated for her 1854 novel *Ruth Hall*), and, at one time, America's highest paid newspaper columnist. During her early schooling at the Hartford Female Academy run by Catherine Beecher, Fern befriended young Harriet Beecher.

stylistic intricacy, psychological subtlety, epistemological complexity – and to see the sentimental novel not as an artifice of eternity answerable to certain formal criteria and to certain psychological and philosophical concerns, but as a political enterprise, halfway between sermon and social theory, that both codifies and attempts to mold the values of its time. [. . .]

Let us consider the episode in *Uncle Tom's Cabin* most often cited as the epitome of Victorian sentimentalism – the death of little Eva – because it is the kind of incident most offensive to the sensibilities of twentieth-century academic critics. It is on the belief that this incident is nothing more than a sob story that the whole case against sentimentalism rests. Little Eva's death, so the argument goes, like every other sentimental tale, is awash with emotion but does nothing to remedy the evils it deplores. Essentially, it leaves the slave system and the other characters unchanged. This trivializing view of the episode is grounded in assumptions about power and reality so common that we are not even aware they are in force. Thus generations of critics have commented with condescending irony on little Eva's death. But in the system of belief that undergirds Stowe's enterprise, dying is the supreme form of heroism. In *Uncle Tom's Cabin*, death is the equivalent not of defeat but of victory; it brings an access of power, not a loss of it; it is not only the crowning achievement of life, it *is* life, and Stowe's entire presentation of little Eva is designed to dramatize this fact.

Stories like the death of little Eva are compelling for the same reason that the story of Christ's death is compelling: they enact a philosophy, as much political as religious, in which the pure and powerless die to save the powerful and corrupt, and thereby show themselves more powerful than those they save. [. . .] The power of the dead or the dying to redeem the unregenerate is a major theme of nineteenth-century popular fiction and religious literature. Mothers and children are thought to be uniquely capable of this work. [. . .] If children because of their purity and innocence can lead adults to God while living, their spiritual power when they are dead is greater still. When the spiritual power of death is combined with the natural sanctity of childhood, the child becomes an angel endowed with salvific force. [. . .]

Of course, it could be argued by critics of sentimentalism that the prominence of stories about the deaths of children is precisely what is wrong with the literature of the period; rather than being cited as a source of strength, the presence of such stories in *Uncle Tom's Cabin* could be regarded as an unfortunate concession to the age's fondness for lachrymose scenes. But to dismiss such scenes as "all tears and flapdoodle" is to leave unexplained the popularity of the novels and sermons that are filled with them, unless we choose to believe that a generation of readers was unaccountably moved to tears by matters that are intrinsically silly and trivial. That popularity is better explained, I believe, by the relationship of these scenes to a pervasive cultural myth which invests the suffering and death of an innocent victim with just the kind of power that critics deny to Stowe's novel: the power to work in, and change, the world.

This is the kind of action that little Eva's death in fact performs. It proves its efficacy not through the sudden collapse of the slave system, but through the conversion of Topsy, a motherless, godless black child who has up until that point successfully resisted all attempts to make her "good." Topsy will not be "good" because, never having had a mother's love, she believes that no one can love her. [. . .] By giving Topsy her love, Eva initiates a process of redemption whose power, transmitted from heart to heart, can change the entire world. [. . .]

If the language of tears seems maudlin and little Eva's death ineffectual, it is because both the tears and the redemption that they signify belong to a conception of the world that is now generally regarded as naive and unrealistic. Topsy's salvation and Miss Ophelia's do not alter the anti-abolitionist majority in the Senate or prevent southern plantation owners and northern investment bankers from doing business to their mutual advantage. Because most modern readers regard such political and economic facts as final, it is difficult for them to take seriously a novel that insists on religious conversion as the necessary precondition for sweeping social change. But in Stowe's understanding of what such change requires, it is the *modern* view that is naive. The political and economic measures that constitute effective action for us, she regards as superficial, mere extensions of the worldly policies that produced the slave system in the first place. Therefore, when Stowe asks the question that is in every reader's mind at the end of the novel – namely, "what can any individual do?" – she recommends not specific alterations in the current political and economic arrangements, but rather a change of heart. [. . .]

Stowe is not opposed to concrete measures such as the passage of laws or the formation of political pressure groups, it is just that, by themselves, such actions would be useless. For if slavery *were* to be abolished by these means, the moral conditions that produced slavery in the first place would continue in force. [. . .] Reality, in Stowe's view, cannot be changed by manipulating the physical environment; it can only be changed by conversion in the spirit because it is the spirit alone that is finally real. [. . .]

Uncle Tom's Cabin retells the culture's central religious myth – the story of the crucifixion – in terms of the nation's greatest political conflict – slavery – and of its most cherished social beliefs – the sanctity of motherhood and the family. It is because Stowe is able to combine so many of the culture's central concerns in a narrative that is immediately accessible to the general population that she is able to move so many people so deeply. [. . .] For the novel functions both as a means of describing the social world and as a means of changing it. It not only offers an interpretive framework for understanding the culture, and, through the reinforcement of a particular code of values, recommends a strategy for dealing with cultural conflict, but it is itself an agent of that strategy, putting into practice the measures it prescribes. [. . .]

Uncle Tom's Cabin, however, unlike its counterparts in the sentimental tradition, was spectacularly persuasive in conventional political terms; it helped convince a nation to go to war and to free its slaves. But in terms of its own conception of power, a conception it shares with other sentimental fiction, the novel was a political failure. Stowe conceived her book as an instrument for bringing about the day when the world would be ruled not by force, but by Christian love. The novel's deepest political aspirations are expressed only secondarily in its devastating attack on the slave system; the true goal of

Stowe's rhetorical undertaking is nothing less than the institution of the kingdom of heaven on earth. [. . .]

One could argue, then, that for all its revolutionary fervor, *Uncle Tom's Cabin* is a conservative book, because it advocates a return to an older way of life – household economy – in the name of the nation's most cherished social and religious beliefs. Even the emphasis on the woman's centrality might be seen as harking back to the "age of homespun" when the essential goods were manu-factured in the home and their production was carried out and guided by women. But Stowe's very conservatism – her reliance on established patterns of living and traditional beliefs – is precisely what gives her novel its revolutionary potential. By pushing those beliefs to an extreme and by insisting that they be applied universally, not just to one segregated corner of civil life, but to the conduct of all human affairs, Stowe means to effect a radical transformation of her society. The brilliance of the strategy is that it puts the central affirmations of a culture into the service of a vision that would destroy the present economic and social institutions; by resting her case, absolutely, on the saving power of Christian love and on the sanctity of motherhood and the family, Stowe relocates the center of power in American life, placing it not in the government, nor in the courts of law, nor in the factories, nor in the marketplace, but in the kitchen. And that means that the new society will not be controlled by men, but by women. [. . .] Male provender is deemphasized in favor of female processing. Men provide the seed, but women bear and raise the children. Men provide the flour, but women bake the bread and get the breakfast. The removal of the male from the center to the periphery of the human sphere is the most radical component of this millenarian scheme, which is rooted so solidly in the most traditional values – religion, motherhood, home, and family. Exactly what position men will occupy in the millennium is specified by a detail inserted casually into Stowe's description of the Indiana kitchen. While the women and children are busy preparing breakfast, Simeon Halliday, the husband and father, stands "in his shirt-sleeves before a little looking-glass in the corner, engaged in the anti-patriarchal operation of shaving" [p. 103].

With this detail, so innocently placed, Stowe reconceives the role of men in human history: while Negroes, children, mothers, and grandmothers do the world's primary work, men groom themselves contentedly in a corner. The scene, as critics have noted is often the case in sentimental fiction, is "intimate," the backdrop is "domestic," the tone at times is even "chatty"; but the import, as critics have failed to recognize, is world-shaking. The enterprise of sentimental fiction, as Stowe's novel attests, is anything but domestic, in the sense of being limited to purely personal concerns. Its mission, on the contrary, is global and its interests identical with the interests of the race. If the fiction written in the nineteenth century by women whose works sold in the hundreds of thousands has seemed narrow and parochial to the critics of the twentieth century, that narrowness and parochialism belong not to these works nor to the women who wrote them; they are the beholders' share.

From **Gillian Brown, *Domestic Individualism: Imagining Self in Nineteenth-Century America*** (Berkeley, Calif.: University of California Press, 1990)

In some ways, Gillian Brown extends and radicalizes Jane Tompkins's ideas. While both feminist critics understand the links between domesticity and political power, Brown claims that *Uncle Tom's Cabin* offers a "critique of conventional domestic ideology as well as an attack on slavery and the marketplace." Slaves in the kitchen disrupt white women's ability to be the morally superior beings that Catherine Beecher promotes in her *Treatise on Domestic Economy* **(pp. 17–18)**. Brown shows how Stowe tries to reform American society by changing domestic values. Brown's arguments most readily apply to Rachel Halliday's Quaker kitchen in Chapter 13 **(pp. 99–104)**, George Harris's dramatic stand in Chapter 11 **(pp. 96–9)**, Cassy's story in Chapter 34 **(pp. 134–8)**.

[. . .] Slavery disregards [the] opposition between the family at home and the exterior workplace. The distinction between work and family is eradicated in the slave, for whom there is no separation between economic and private status. When people themselves are "articles" subject to "mercantile dealings," when "the souls and bodies of men" are "equivalent to money," women can no longer keep houses that provide a refuge from marketplace activities. Slavery, according to *Uncle Tom's Cabin*, undermines women's housework by bringing the confusion of the marketplace into the kitchen, the center of the family shelter. The real horror that slavery holds for the mothers of America to whom Stowe addressed her anti-slavery appeal is the suggestion that the family life nurtured by women is not immune to the economic life outside it.

In fashioning her abolitionist protest as a defense of nineteenth-century domestic values, Stowe designates slavery as a domestic issue for American women to adjudicate and manage. The call to the mothers of America for the abolition of slavery is a summons to fortify the home, to rescue domesticity from shiftlessness and slavery. [. . .]

Tompkins's account of sentimental power offers an important reevaluation of sentimentalism [. . .] But Tompkins's argument for *Uncle Tom's Cabin*'s literary value as a "political enterprise" overlooks the fact that Stowe's polemic for a regenerating domesticity is a critique of conventional domestic ideology as well as an attack on slavery and the marketplace. What makes *Uncle Tom's Cabin* a particularly striking domestic novel is that Stowe seeks to reform American society not by employing domestic values but by reforming them. The domestic ideology from which *Uncle Tom's Cabin* derives its reformative force is, when understood historically, a patriarchal institution. The novel addresses this relation between patriarchy and sentimental ideals by explicitly thematizing the intimacy and congress between economic and domestic endeavors, between market and kitchen systems. Therefore the domesticity Stowe advocates must be understood as a revision and purification of popular domestic values – domestic values which Stowe regards as complicit with the patriarchal institution of slavery. Stowe's domestic solution to slavery, then, represents not the strength of sentimental values but a utopian rehabilitation of them, necessitated by their fundamental complicity with the market to which they are ostensibly opposed. [. . .]

The ideal kitchen in *Uncle Tom's Cabin* functions smoothly under the aegis of "motherly loving kindness" [**p. 101**]. Rachel Halliday's kitchen in the Indiana Quaker settlement that shelters runaway slaves is, like Ophelia's, "without a particle of dust"; but more than orderliness, its "rows of shining tins, suggestive of unmentionable good things to the appetite," indicate the value of abundance and generosity in Stowe's utopian domestic economy [**p. 100**]. Ophelia, Stowe explains in her *Key to Uncle Tom's Cabin*, despite her "activity, zeal, unflinching conscientiousness, clear intellectual discriminations between truth and error, and great logical and doctrinal correctness," "represents one great sin": the lack of the Christian "spirit of love." Rachel embodies and dispenses that spirit of love, "diffusing a sort of sunny radiance" over meal preparations. Making breakfast under Rachel's supervision is "like picking up the rose-leaves and trimming the bushes in Paradise," a vision of perfect, happy labor [**p. 103**]. "There was so much motherliness and full-heartedness even in the way she passed a plate of cakes or poured a cup of coffee, that it seemed to put a spirit into the food and drink she offered" [**p. 103**]. Rachel's domestic acts appear sacramental, her meals a communion reminiscent of Edenic unity:

> Everything went on so sociably, so quietly, so harmoniously, in the great kitchen, – it seemed so pleasant to everyone to do just what they were doing, there was such an atmosphere of mutual confidence and good-fellowship everywhere, – even the knives and forks had a social clatter as they went on the table; and the chicken and ham had a cheerful and joyous fizzle in the pan, as if they enjoyed being cooked. [**p. 103**]

The spirit of mother-love creates a domesticity in the image of paradise: a world before separations, a domestic economy before markets.

Eliza, Harry, and George Harris, the runaway slaves reunited in the Halliday sentimental utopia, discover that "[t]his, indeed, was a home, – *home* – a word that [they] had never yet known a meaning for" [**p. 103**]. Rachel's "simple, over-flowing kindness" defines the perfect home, and that kindness includes helping runaway slaves. This defiance of the Fugitive Slave Law[1] demonstrates the commitment of the Quaker community to God's love and familial feeling over man's law. In Rachel's kitchen the boys and girls share domestic duties under their mother's guidance while their father engages in "the anti-patriarchal operation of shaving" [**p. 103**]. Godlike mothers generate and rule this family state by their love. In Stowe's model home, domesticity is matriarchal and antinomian, a new

---

1   The Fugitive Slave Law of 1850 made it illegal for northerners to assist runaway slaves; therefore, in serving dinner to George, Eliza, and Harry, Rachel Halliday breaks the federal law.

form of government as well as a protest against patriarchy and its manifestations in slavery, capitalism, and democracy. Her domestic advice carries an addendum to the household practices Beecher assigned to women: the duty of women to oppose slavery and the law that upholds it.

"It's a shameful, wicked, abominable law," Mrs. Bird, another concerned housekeeper in *Uncle Tom's Cabin*, tells her senator husband, "and I shall break it, the first time I get a chance" [p. 91]. She gets her chance when Eliza collapses in the Bird kitchen after she escapes from Kentucky by crossing the frozen Ohio River. *Uncle Tom's Cabin* politicizes women's domestic role at the very moment of sentimentalizing that role, urging women to stop slavery, in the name of love. Love and protest, maternal duty and political action, compose Stowe's reformulated domestic virtue. [. . .]

This notion of femininity as maternal, literary, political, and mystical conjoins domestic and feminist values, incorporating both self-denial and self-assertion in the ideal woman. *Uncle Tom's Cabin* retains the Christian domestic tenet of feminine self-abnegation in order to elaborate a maternal power commensurate to the task of abolishing slavery. [. . .] This religious interpretation of ideal maternal practices merges motherhood with Christianity. The self-sacrifice of women or slaves, then, signifies redemption and eternal life. *Uncle Tom's Cabin* allies this conventional feminine mode with the civil disobedience of Rachel and Mrs. Bird and the dramatic escapes from slavery, first by Eliza and then by Cassy, that comprise the activist female model Stowe proposes. For Stowe, domestic self-denial and feminist self-seeking can be complementary manners. [. . .]

Stowe's rejection of the masculine political economy finds its most explicit and emphatic expression in George Harris's renunciation of America and filial duty to its laws: "I haven't any country, any more than I have a father." When commanded by his master to forget his marriage to Eliza and to cohabit with another slave woman, George runs away to Canada, "where the laws will own . . . and protect" him. He wants the familial structure he has been denied since childhood, the company of the mother and sisters from whom he was separated. Despising the values of his white male ancestry, George chooses the feminine economy of mother-love: "My sympathies are not for my father's race, but for my mother's. To him I was no more than a fine dog or horse: to my poor heart-broken mother I was a *child*" [p. 147]. To defend the familial relation, the rights of women as it were, George seeks another country. [. . .]

Stowe replaces the master–slave relation with the benign proprietorship of mother–child, transferring the ownership of slaves to the mothers of America. Women prefer familial ties to market relations, caring for the welfare of their dependents – children and slaves – rather than for the profits wrought from them. In Stowe's matriarchal society, slaves are synonymous with children because they lack title to themselves and need abolitionist guardianship – which is to say, maternal aid. Maternal supervision, the ideal form of owning in Stowe's reformed property relations, follows the pattern of divine care. [. . .] By imitating God's parental economy, mothers approximate heaven in their homes. [. . .]

The landscape of Simon Legree's plantation, the last Southern residence Stowe describes, seems more foreign and fantastic than heaven because it is completely nondomestic, unkempt, and ungoverned. [. . .]

Here Tom meets Cassy, the slave woman with plans for freedom that do not involve martyrdom. Very much an actress in human affairs rather than divine or supernatural ones, Cassy confronts the issue of how to find temporal power in femininity and slavery. Cassy, kept for the pleasure of her various owners, signifies the other side of domesticity or, rather, life without the romance and virtue of domesticity. In contrast to the ideals of family unity and redemptive death embodied in Mrs. Shelby, Eliza, Rachel, and Eva, Cassy's experience dramatizes the condition of domestic violation unrelieved by Christian hope, a darker version of Eliza's plight. [. . .]

But the fact that Stowe retains the name of the male God throughout her matriarchal design suggests that her imagination of a feminized world still requires the sanction of male authority, or at least of the modes associated with masculine power. Her utopian female dominion seems uncannily familiar, not only because it invokes popular domestic ideals, but because it resembles masculine practices of power. Stowe borrows from patriarchal authority the prerogative of dispatching human destinies, the same prerogative exercised by men and slave-masters. Finally, violence in *Uncle Tom's Cabin* not only is executed by the slave economy and masculine desire that endanger the family and home but is embedded in the very foundation of the home. For Stowe, only a house divided, a house divested of men, markets, and desire, can be a home.

From **Lawrence Buell, *New England Literary Culture: From Revolution Through Renaissance*** (New York, N.Y.: Cambridge University Press, 1986)

By discussing Stowe's treatment of Scripture and by her identifying Uncle Tom as "The Martyr" (Chapter 40, pp. 138–41), Buell highlights the significance of a Christian vision to the novel's thematic, political, and religious concerns.

Altogether, a good deal of what is most challenging and memorable in the literature of New England between 1770 and 1860 arises from the interplay, often within the same work, between the voices of the believer, the seeker, the skeptic, and the virtuoso. This interplay becomes increasingly complex, self-conscious, and (as non-Christian mythography is introduced) broad-ranging, proof of the Thoreauvian maxim that "decayed literature makes the richest of all soils."

Nowhere is this more evident than in the case of the most spectacular product of the religious imagination in antebellum New England, Harriet Beecher Stowe's *Uncle Tom's Cabin*. The commercial success of this novel, which outsold its nearest rivals in popular fiction by a margin of three to one, warns us again not to envisage the stages of literary scripturism as a simple linear sequence. Such writers as Melville, Thoreau, and Dickinson represent the literary avant-garde but not the net cultural outcome of the religious tendencies of the period. [. . .] Historians of

American religion have shown, for example, that evangelicalism and church membership dramatically increased during the early nineteenth century, at the very time when the higher criticism was taking hold in elite circles. [. . .]

[Stowe's] writing is equally valuable as an exhibit of the ferment within the precincts of orthodoxy itself that, in the long run, pushed Christian evangelicalism [. . .] even while appealing to and seeming to promote old-fashioned, Bible-centered Christianity. Up to a point, *Uncle Tom's Cabin* is a traditional jeremiad. It assaults institutionalized religion, as Puritan fast-day sermons did, by invoking against it the vision of a true and purified holy commonwealth, arguing from a review of the signs of the times that its spiritual pathology can be cured only by religious revival. But the book finally calls for something closer to revolution than to restoration, insofar as it finds the true sources of spiritual renewal and authority on society's margins – in women, children, and blacks – and insofar as the religion of the heart that such people exemplify for Stowe represents a challenge to the patriarchal theological establishment. Stowe was by no means the sole or first voice in the movement toward the "domestication of theology," whereby the stern, masculine God of justice was modified into a feminized God of mercy, and the glittering but remote abstraction of heaven was redefined in terms of the warm, intimate image of home. But Stowe might at least be credited with having produced "the *summa theologica* of nineteenth-century America's religion of domesticity."[1]

The boldness of her prophetic imagination is shown most strikingly in her treatment of Scripture, which she reverenced but which, like every good feminist and antislavery advocate, she knew she also had to challenge. And she did not take the easy route of haggling over the Pauline passages that counsel acquiescence to slavery as the law of the land or admonish women to keep silent in church. "This novel," as Jane Tompkins says, "does not simply quote the Bible, it rewrites the Bible." Stowe is led, for example, to create the first fictional Christ figure in American literature, in the person of Uncle Tom, whom she carefully feminizes as a "Victorian heroine: pious, domestic, self-sacrificing, emotionally uninhibited in response to people and ethical questions." As in the New Testament, a book of Acts follows the passion narrative. Tom's very literal crucifixion leads causally to his young master George Shelby's conversion to abolitionism and symbolically to the evangelization of Africa by the surviving black characters. They then start to carry out the millennial vision intimated long before of Africa's future rise to greatness as the race most likely to develop Christian virtues to perfection (owing to its characteristic traits of trustingness and humility). Thus Stowe brings about the triple triumph of Christianity, Africa, and the feminine, and with this the humbling of American spiritual pride, not only through the book-long indictment of slavery but through her neat reversal of the ideology of American manifest destiny – the debased residue of the Puritan and Revolutionary conception of American chosenness.

---

1   The phrase is Jane Tompkins's. See the extract from her essay "Sentimental Power: *Uncle Tom's Cabin* and the Politics of Literary History," on **p. 44**.

Like any author, Stowe must have been unaware of some of her book's ideological implications. In conceiving the plight and destiny of women and blacks as interrelated examples of the Christian idea that the humble shall be exalted, Stowe made it easy to conceal from herself the full extent of her ambivalence toward blacks (whom she could not comfortably accept as fellow American citizens) and toward the rights of women (whom she sees, conservatively, as influencing society through moral suasion rather than through the political process). At least the novel shows no recognition that its proposed solutions would, if implemented, leave any legitimate unmet need or demand out of account. [. . .]

In *Uncle Tom's Cabin* [. . .] the theory and practice of religion tend to boil down to a single imperative: People must do what "they feel right" [**p. 150**]. [. . .] But the boiling-down process remained emotionally powerful – as the reception of *Uncle Tom* shows – so long as entrenched orthodoxies remained with which to do battle, either without or within. In such a climate, religious literature, which almost by definition complements, if it does not oppose, theological discourse by relying on affective appeal rather than cognition, is bound to flourish. And in mid-nineteenth-century America, as Stowe found, to her amazement, it flourished sufficiently to help ensure the transformation of civil strife into holy war.

From **Susan Gillman, "The Squatter, the Don, and the Grandissimes in Our America,"** in *Mixing Race, Mixing Culture: Inter-American Literary Dialogues*, eds. Monika Kaup and Debra J. Rosenthal (Austin, Tex.: University of Texas Press, 2002)

José Martí (1853–95) is considered Cuba's great liberator: he fought diligently to free Cuba from Spain's totalitarian rule. He also was a prominent intellectual, poet, playwright, and political essayist. As an influential man of letters, Martí admired *Uncle Tom's Cabin* and linked Stowe to U.S. poet, novelist, and Indian rights activist Helen Hunt Jackson (1830–85), who, in her 1884 novel *Ramona*, aimed to raise awareness of Native Americans' plight just as Stowe raised awareness of slaves' plight. Susan Gillman discusses the implications of linking these two novels: slaves and Native Americans became linked as similarly oppressed groups, thus uniting two reform movements.

Known throughout the nineteenth century primarily as the author of *Uncle Tom's Cabin*, Martí's Stowe is something more. Rather than standing alone, for Martí she is always invoked in the same breath as Helen Hunt Jackson, author of *Ramona*, the 1884 romance of Indian reform, one of five novels Martí translated into Spanish. Martí's Stowe has a twin, then in Jackson. *Ramona*, Martí says in the introduction to his 1887 translation, speaks out in favor of the Indians as Harriet Beecher Stowe did for the Negroes [. . .]

For Martí, however, the point of pairing Stowe with Jackson is less to rank the

relative merits of the two reformist writers than to bring together the two
oppressed groups for which they speak. [. . .] Martí's composite figure of Stowe-
and-Jackson links the world-famous North American abolitionist with the
nationally prominent spokeswoman for the Indian cause, bringing together what
are in the U.S. the distinctly separate reform movements of the Negro and the
Indian [. . .]

As a writer both of the abolitionist novel and the romance of Indian reform,
Martí's Stowe–Jackson is greater then the sum of her parts: she becomes an inter-
ethnic, international figure capable of speaking to both the limits and possibilities
of the multiple racial and national aspirations of Latin America and the
Caribbean. [. . .] A black–Indian connection, à la Martí, emerges to address, even
to reveal and formulate, the following puzzles in late nineteenth-century
American literary history: why did the post-Reconstruction era witness the
emergence of parallel, but unremarked, vogues for the "local color" of two
regions, the Old South and the Southwest? How do the parallel "fantasy heri-
tages" associated with both regions map national history onto transnational
geographies?

Associating the so-called "Negro and Indian Questions" in ways virtually
unheard of in the U.S. context, where those terms originate, Martí's Stowe, with
her twin Jackson, represents his remaking of the North American "woman's"
tradition of sentimentalist reform and romantic racialism in the image of "our
mestizo America." [. . .]

Martí's mestiza Stowe–Jackson brings together what are in the U.S. separate
reform movements; if abolitionism preceded, and perhaps preempted, the
emergence of a viable Indian reform movement, by the 1880s, the increasing
presence of the Indian Question – the disappearing Indian – on the national
political and cultural agenda must be balanced against what amounts to a
nearly opposite movement, supported by the law and medico-scientific thinking,
to erase – by legalized segregation or theories of black degeneracy and biological inferiority – the Negro Question from the national consciousness. In
contrast, however, Martí's Stowe–Jackson insists on thinking of the two questions
as one.

From **Amy Schrager Lang, *Prophetic Woman: Anne Hutchinson and
the Problem of Dissent in the Literature of New England*** (Berkeley,
Calif.: University of California Press, 1987)

In this excerpt, Lang discusses the importance of virtues traditionally viewed
as Christian, especially those of passivity and submissiveness, to Stowe's
conception of race and gender in *Uncle Tom's Cabin*. Women and slaves, Lang
shows, prove to be ideal Christians because of their passivity, and hence are
stronger morally. Lang refers to the Fugitive Slave Act of 1850 which effectively
brought slavery and its laws to the North: northerners were forbidden by the
Act to help runaway slaves.

In 1852 Harriet Beecher Stowe urged the readers of *Uncle Tom's Cabin* to "feel right" and to oppose slavery. As Stowe presents them, these are synonymous: to consult feeling is to discover Christian truth written upon the heart; to oppose the Fugitive Slave Act is to choose Christ and to repudiate the world. Although Stowe directed her appeal to men and women alike, *Uncle Tom's Cabin* – a novel governed by distinctions of race and gender and written at a moment when "woman's fiction" dominated the American literary marketplace – not surprisingly insists upon the moral superiority of women. By nature and circumstance, Stowe suggests, women are more likely to "feel right" and are, therefore, less willing than men to tolerate the legalized horrors of slavery. The most virtuous women in *Uncle Tom's Cabin* are those who rely most fully on the heart to guide them. Setting a private, unassailable, and deeply felt knowledge of God's truth against the cruelty and corruption of a world governed by men, these women hold the promise of a future without slavery. [. . .]

By saying that the domestic novel idealizes the status quo, I do not mean that it simply ratifies what is. There is a middle term in the transformation of the domestic heroine: she comes to terms with the world around her by becoming a Christian. Reading her Bible, she discovers a private truth, witnessed by God and attested to by her heart. But that discovery, rather than pitting her against the world, transforms her into a model for its improvement. The feminine interior self reiterates ideal Christian values, which, in turn, replicate the highest principles of society, though not necessarily the principles we see at work there. [. . .]

"The object of these sketches," Stowe explains in the preface to *Uncle Tom's Cabin*, "is to awaken sympathy and feeling for the African race, as they exist among us; to show their wrongs and sorrows, under a system so necessarily cruel and unjust as to defeat . . . all that can be attempted for them . . . under it" [p. 83]. Once exposed, however, the injustice of slavery must necessarily be opposed. Pitting divine law, revealed as feeling, against civil law, Stowe argues, that to violate the law of the state – in this case, the Fugitive Slave Act – is to uphold the law of the feminine heart. [. . .]

[T]he novel's vision of the world once reformed is clear. It will look like the home, or rather it will look like the matriarchal Quaker settlement, which, in its profound isolation from the marketplace and its perfect domesticity, is the home writ large. Only during our brief glimpse of the matriarch Rachel Halliday and the community of Friends over which she reigns in the paradise of Indiana do we escape the contradictions inherent in Stowe's appeal to feminine feeling to end slavery. Elsewhere, the pattern of conflict that characterizes Stowe's portrayal of the Shelbys is repeated with increasing force. In the chapter "In Which It Appears That a Senator is But a Man," for example, the coincidence of feminine virtue with feminine powerlessness narrowly circumscribes the influence of the devout Mrs. Bird. Horrified at her husband's support of the Fugitive Slave Act, Mrs. Bird invokes what is "right and Christian" in an effort to counter her husband's insistence that slavery is not a matter of "private feeling" but of "great public interests." Humanity and Christianity are, of course, on Mrs. Bird's side, but her virtue is explicitly represented as depending on her exclusion from the realm of public affairs. "I don't know anything about politics," she exclaims, "but I can read my Bible and there I see that I must feed the hungry, clothe the naked, and comfort the desolate, and that Bible I mean to follow" [p. 91].

Seen one way, the implication of this statement is that if she did know anything about politics, Biblical injunctions might be overridden by interest. Mrs. Bird's moral rectitude, as her husband points out, is, like Mrs. Shelby's, a luxury of dependence: she has no constituency to please, no bread to win. The moral purity of her stance is assured by her exclusion from the world of politics. [. . .] The Bird episode is designed to speak directly to the collision of private feeling and public action. Stowe addresses this conflict by drawing a distinction between Mr. Bird, the private man, and Senator Bird, the public official. Summoned to aid Eliza and Harry, Mr. Bird acts out of feeling and acquits himself admirably, restoring in the process his wife's faith in his humanity. But as far as we know, this act of private charity – which, not incidentally, violates the very law he has helped to enact – has no effect whatsoever on his public posture. At home, the man partakes of the virtues the home represents. Removed from public view, the domestic sphere fosters the best of the private self – by definition, a feminine self. But the actions of the senator are dictated by the "public interests" that hedge him in on all sides. By turning to Mr. Bird in her effort to resolve the seemingly irresolvable conflict between private and public values, Stowe rescues intact the separate spheres of men and women. More important, she establishes the existence of an inner, feminine self in men that makes them, like women, susceptible to moral suasion. [. . .]

Unlike her father, little Eva is a character disabled by both age and sex. Too good to grow into adulthood in a world where Christian love is defeated at every turn by the brutality of slavery, Eva dies not of disease but of an excess of feeling. In her fatal empathy as in other respects, her virtues magnify and perfect those of the other women in the novel: too young to be a mother, Eva's dealings with Topsy nonetheless mimic the best of mothering; like the model Mrs. Bird, she abhors violence of any sort; with Mrs. Shelby, she longs to protect the weak and the helpless. Loyal, generous, self-denying, and faithful, Eva would if she could grow up to become the exemplary wife and mother. In fact, one proof of the evil of slavery is that it requires the sacrifice of Eva, at once a female Christ and a new Eve.

As others have shown, Eva's feminine virtue and her spotless death are repeated, in color, one might say, in Uncle Tom. She dies, pale and peaceful, in her lily-white bed while he is beaten to death in Legree's shed. [. . .] Yet [they] share the essential qualities of the heroine of domestic fiction: they are pious, submissive, self-sacrificing, and affectionate. [. . .] Allied by their powerlessness and their virtue, Tom and Eva are, of course, the most powerful characters in the novel. Evangelists both, bringing the good news of mankind's redemption through Christ, their deaths finalize the opposition between slavery and domestic Christianity and hold out hope for the future. [. . .]

In the first half of Uncle Tom's Cabin we move in an orderly progress from one domestic setting to another – from the Shelbys to the Birds to the Hallidays –

building toward the false hope of an Augustine St. Clare. With St. Clare's death we are left desolate in the wilderness with Tom, the most completely powerless and, as we learn, for that reason the most powerful character in the novel. Unlike the frail, pale St. Clare, Uncle Tom is a "large, broad-chested, powerfully made man of a full glossy black," capable of picking a double-weight of cotton to relieve his fellow slave. In him, femininity is a wholly interior attribute, signified by his extreme blackness and variously expressed as empathy, affection, domesticity, and humility. Tom's femininity, unlike St. Clare's, is bound not to poetic temperament but to religious faith. Feminized and disempowered by slavery, Tom cannot, of course, act. What he can do, as he tells Legree, is die and, by dying, reenact Christ's sacrifice. [. . .]

George Shelby, about whose character we know nothing beyond his adolescent attachment to Tom, is reborn at Tom's graveside as the liberator St. Clare once imagined himself. Filled with guilt and righteous anger, he calls on God to "witness, that, from this hour, I will do *what one man can* to drive out this curse of slavery from my land!" [**p. 144**]. What he can do, of course, is free his slaves, and he returns immediately to Kentucky to do just that. [. . .]

Ultimately, then, the domestic ideology that underlies *Uncle Tom's Cabin* cannot translate feminine feeling into masculine deed. Consequently, the solution to slavery the novel offers is not social but individual, not political but spiritual, not public but private. Insisting on the moral superiority of the disempowered – wives, mothers, and slaves – *Uncle Tom's Cabin* moves, as it must, beyond the home wherein the powerless are guaranteed their virtue and the virtuous their lack of power. But it moves not out to the world of men but up to heaven, the perfect and eternal home.

It is, of course, only in heaven that the feminine can safely and completely supplant the masculine, but the fact that Stowe abandons the social for the religious does not mean that the novel's strategy fails in political terms. In fact, the tremendous impact of *Uncle Tom's Cabin* is bound to its substitution of the language of gender for that of politics. Removing the problem of slavery from the public to the private sphere, transforming it from a problem of state to one of individual faith, this substitution allows women – in fact, Stowe herself – to recall the nation to its own ideals and transforms the novel into a Jeremiad. On the one hand, enlisting the ideological conventions of the domestic novel in opposition to slavery, Stowe demonstrates that its terms prohibit the move from private feeling to public forms of redress and, thus, contains the lawlessness potential in opposition to slavery. On the other hand, empowering the domestic virtue of women, she calls America not to rebellion but to Christ. Addressing her reader out of the shared experience of maternity – "And oh!, mother that reads this, has there never been in your house a drawer . . . the opening of which has been to you like the opening . . . of a little grave?" – she appeals as a woman to other women to "feel right" and pray.

From **Marianne Noble, "The Ecstasies of Sentimental Wounding in *Uncle Tom's Cabin*"** in *The Masochistic Pleasures of Sentimental Literature* (Princeton, N.J.: Princeton University Press, 2000)

What is the link between pleasure and pain? In this extract, Marianne Noble suggests that the numerous scenes of pain in *Uncle Tom's Cabin* actually give readers a certain pleasure, not unlike the way we as drivers take a perverse pleasure in slowing down to view the horrors of a car accident. Noble theorizes the coincidence of sentiment, eroticism, and pain in *Uncle Tom's Cabin* and what it meant for the nineteenth-century woman reader.

Harriet Beecher Stowe's *Uncle Tom's Cabin* [is] a paradigm of nineteenth-century sentimentality and an indisputably important political novel. Nowhere are the complications of a nineteenth-century woman's exploitation of sentimental masochism for power and pleasure more vividly displayed. Stowe sought to make readers feel the pain that slaves felt in order to force upon them an intuitive, experiential approach to the abolitionist question. Taking advantage of conventional sentimental strategies, she deliberately inflicted emotional wounds and urged readers to identify the pain of these wounds with the suffering of slaves, so that they would *feel* the urgency of the abolitionist cause. Her motive for this political activism was fundamentally religious; she wanted to show that African Americans had souls and a spiritual dimension and to oppose the affront to Christianity represented by slavery. As feminist critics of the past twenty years have observed, Stowe's Christian politics represented a radical feminist intervention into, and critique of, American public life. What they have not recognized, however, is that the contextualization of Stowe's painful sentimental affect within Christian and racial discourses had the effect of eroticizing that affect.

Many readers have confessed that the reading of *Uncle Tom's Cabin* stimulated masochistic erotic desires. In "A Child Is Being Beaten," Sigmund Freud observes that many patients have beating fantasies, and many of them use *Uncle Tom's Cabin* for "onanistic gratification": "In my patients' milieu it was almost always the same books whose contents gave a new stimulus to the beating-phantasies: those accessible to young people, such as the so-called '*Bibliothèque rose*,' *Uncle Tom's Cabin*, etc." In her study of masochistic desire, Marcia Marcus lists the childhood books that provided materials for her own adolescent masochistic fantasies: "There were the books about boarding school, in which small boys slaved for the bigger boys. ... There were books about the initiation rites of exotic people. There was *Uncle Tom's Cabin*, and other books about black slaves in America. There were books about armies with iron discipline and military justice and punitive expeditions."[1] Likewise, Richard Krafft-Ebing,[2] the sex

---

1 [Noble's note.] Marcia Marcus, *A Taste for Pain: On Masochism and Female Sexuality*, trans. Joan Tate (New York, N.Y.: St. Martin's, 1981).
2 Richard Krafft-Ebing (1840–1902), was a German physician and neurologist considered an authority on deviant sexual behavior.

researcher who coined the term "masochism," includes in his compendium on sexual pathology the following letter from a self-diagnosed masochist (Case 57): "Even in my early childhood I loved to revel in ideas about the absolute mastery of one man over others. The thought of slavery had something exciting in it for me, alike whether from the standpoint of master or servant. That one man could possess, sell or whip another, caused me intense excitement; and in reading 'Uncle Tom's Cabin' (which I read at about the beginning of puberty) I had erections." Case 57 adds that "there are many men who like to play 'slave' . . . this unlimited power of life and death, as exercised over slaves and domestic animals, is the aim and end of all masochistic ideas."

In this [essay] I illuminate the complex mechanisms by which *Uncle Tom's Cabin* came to function as such a notoriously successful supply of material for masochistic erotic fantasy; readers who read about the transcendent pleasures of mystical martyrdom and interracial bonding and who also felt the gut response typical of sentimental affect frequently associated sentimental pain with pleasures of a private erotic or ecstatic character rather than with disinterested altruistic desires to serve the public good. *Uncle Tom's Cabin* came to function as such a notoriously successful supply of material for masochistic erotic fantasy. I also address the ethical and political implications of the popularity of *Uncle Tom's Cabin* as masochistic fantasy: the pleasures it creates call into question its appropriateness as political discourse, and yet these pleasures played a key role in the popularity of the book that President Lincoln believed started the Civil War,[3] a war that resulted in the emancipation of the slaves. Power and pleasure turn in upon themselves in *Uncle Tom's Cabin*, making a final judgment of the ethics of sentimental masochism as a mode of agency all but impossible.

Stowe turned to sentimentalism not to please readers but to promote her own political position: sentimentalism was a tool of political agency. But the book was powerful at least in part because of the illicit pleasures it produced. Readers turned to it – and to the cause it promoted – because of the pleasures associated with its production of sympathy. Though its sadomasochistic tendencies made the book politically effective, they also undermined the spiritual goals that motiv-ated Stowe to write it in the first place. For the sadomasochistic pleasures that made her book so powerful also positioned the slaves as erotic objects rather than fully human subjects. And her spiritual goal – to recognize the humanity and spirituality of slaves – was undermined by that objectification, even as the political goal was energized as never before.

From the perspective of feminism as well as that of abolitionism, the implica-tions of sentimental masochism are double-edged. Women, Stowe suggests through her novel, needed to reform the dehumanizing male-dominated political system through a spiritually motivated platform of sympathy and feelings. Yet by effectively promoting suffering as women's most significant form of political agency, *Uncle Tom's Cabin* cut against more affirmative and proactive forms of

---

3   When Stowe visited President Abraham Lincoln at the White House in Washington, D.C. in 1862, he reportedly greeted her by stating, "So you're the little woman who wrote the book that started this great war."

women's empowerment. Moreover, while eroticized suffering conveniently made passion accessible to middle-class women for whom ideologies of true woman-hood and Calvinism rendered passion taboo, it also oppressively suggested that suffering was the central component of a distinctly female variety of sexual pleasure. Because of the high stakes involved in the double-edgedness of its senti-mental masochistic erotics, *Uncle Tom's Cabin* offers a uniquely dramatic example of the complexities attending the pursuit of a voice of female pleasure and power.

In order to forge between readers and slaves a union based upon shared feelings, [Stowe] reinvigorates readers' own anguished memories of bereavement and separation, suggesting that those experiences are qualitatively the same as the miseries of slavery. [. . .] [Senator Bird's] approach epitomizes prevailing epistemologies; he supports the Fugitive Slave Law because he thinks in de-humanizing abstractions, such as "fugitives," and never considers the emotions of the human beings represented by these abstractions: "his idea of a fugitive was only an idea of the letters that spell the word, – or at the most, the image of a little newspaper picture of a man with a stick and bundle with 'Ran away from the subscriber' under it. The magic of the real presence of distress, – the imploring human eye, the frail, trembling human hand, the despairing appeal of helpless agony, – these he had never tried." He is reformed by a sentimental wound. When Eliza Harris attempts to explain why she ran away from the Shelbys, she interrupts the senator's series of logical questions with a question of her own that shifts the epistemological basis of the discussion. She asks if the Birds have ever lost a child, a question that was "thrust on a new wound." When the Birds answer yes, Eliza explains "Then you will feel for me. I have lost two" [p. 93]. This fictional example illustrates Stowe's own literary method: she thrusts into readers' preexisting wounds, forcing them to "feel for" slaves by reexperiencing their own painful separations and other forms of suffering. This wounding forces a new mode of cognition upon readers, who are to understand slavery through their memories of sorrow rather than through reason, and thereby apprehend the "plain right thing" that logic conceals.

In the climactic whipping scene in *Uncle Tom's Cabin*, wounding is so intim-ately linked with desire that torture seems to express longing and intensity of imagined pleasure more than it does literal physical agony. When a fellow slave taunts Tom that he is about to be whipped to death, Stowe writes, "The savage words none of them reached that ear! – a higher voice there was saying, 'Fear not them that kill the body, and, after that, have no more that they can do.' Nerve and bone of that poor man's body vibrated to those words, as if touched by the finger of God; and he felt the strength of a thousand souls in one. . . . His soul throbbed, – his home was in sight, – and the hour of release seemed at hand." As Stowe casts about for powerful imagery to express the desire for "real presence," a desire that is at the heart of these climactic scenes, she turns to a number of words that seem sexual, particularly when they appear together in the same passage: "throbbed," "release," "vibrated," "touched by the finger," "joy and desire." Sexual desire, like religious desire, is frequently about a longing for the other's "real presence," not simply proximity nor simply emotional or intellectual connection. And this convergence, in the climax of the novel, of sexual language with notions of a desire for real presence, condensed in the trope of the wound, may well explain why *Uncle Tom's Cabin* provided the foundation for the masturbation fantasies quoted at the head of this chapter. Readers experienced the book as a kind of emotional wounding; Stowe identified her strategy as one of thrusting into readers' wounds, and associates wounds with sexualized expressions of ecstatic transcendence. Readers therefore were in a good position to experience the textual affect as a form of sexual transcendence. While literary history abounds with descriptions of innocents suffering cruelty and violent subjugation, few books feature the convergence of ecstatic transcendence, sexual language, and sadistic torture as vividly as does *Uncle Tom's Cabin*.

The love for the slave is not entirely chaste. [. . .] Eva urges her father to buy Tom because, as she puts it, "I want him" [**p. 106**]. The desire of the white woman for the black man is a cliché in America; barred by race from bourgeois respectability, African Americans have traditionally been mythologized as supersexual beings associated with tropical heat, fire, blood, and strength. [. . .] Feminizing and emasculating [male slaves] frees [Stowe] to desire them, for as tortured objects of pity, they invite the full force of love, tenderness, and longing for intimacy that Stowe could never bestow upon a black man represented as subject. Projecting masochistic desires onto these powerfully sensual (but sentimentalized) figures eroticizes the identification that unites two people in the bonds of one sorrow.

From **Jim O'Loughlin, "Articulating *Uncle Tom's Cabin*,"** *New Literary History*, 31 (2000): 573–97

> In this insightful discussion of Topsy, Jim O'Loughlin analyzes Stowe's strategies in figuring Topsy as an unruly slave child put into the reforming, molding hands of Miss Ophelia, a white northerner. This selection especially refers to Chapter 20 of *Uncle Tom's Cabin* (**pp. 112–20**).

[. . .] Topsy appears midway through Stowe's novel when St. Clare buys the slave child in order to put Miss Ophelia's educational and anti-slavery theories to a practical test. He intentionally picks the physically battered and seemingly incorrigible Topsy because he feels Ophelia's methods will not work on a brutalized child of slavery. [. . .] St. Clare is proven correct as Ophelia's methods prove incapable of training Topsy, whose stealing, lying, and general demeanor disrupt life in the St. Clare household. In fact, Ophelia's own antipathy toward blacks stands in the way of changing Topsy's behavior. Only Eva's genuine love and affection is able to have an effect on Topsy. Once convinced that Eva cares for her, Topsy begins to change her ways, and Eva's death causes her to strive to be good. [. . .]

In Stowe's account, what is most intriguing about Topsy is that she is a character without a personal narrative. As Ophelia's initial questioning of her reveals, Topsy knows nothing of her age, her parents, conceptions of time, or God. When asked by Ophelia if she knows who made her, Topsy replies "I spect I grow'd. Don't think nobody never made me" [p. 115]. It is partly this lack of a personal narrative that explains Topsy's function within slavery as a commodity. Without connections to anyone or any place, Topsy herself seems to care little whose possession she is. Topsy's situation provides a telling comparison with that of Uncle Tom. Uncle Tom's tragedy is that he does have a personal narrative, a family, and a past he is forced to leave, and as such he can appreciate personally the ramifications of being a slave. Topsy's initial tragedy is that she has no basis from which to oppose her situation. She cannot envision any alternative to her commodified existence within slavery.

As a character without a personal narrative, Topsy has little to guide and shape her actions. Topsy infuriates Ophelia by stealing small household items, such as gloves, ribbons, and earrings. Yet the objects mean nothing to Topsy. When Ophelia tells her to admit her thefts or face a whipping, Topsy confesses to all she took and, for good measure, admits to taking Eva's necklace as well, even though it was never stolen. Similarly, Topsy's random appropriation of behaviors from others can be seen as a substitute for her lack of a personal narrative: "Her talent for every species of drollery, grimace, and mimicry – for dancing, tumbling, climbing, singing, whistling, imitating every sound that hit her fancy – seemed inexhaustible." Yet this talent, like the objects she takes, fails to influence her actions meaningfully. The problem of Topsy, as presented by Stowe, is that she is a character without character, a site where different discourses converge, but which have no influence in shaping her.

Topsy's subsequent story concerns how Eva's individual affection gives her a narrative and a past. When Eva confronts Topsy as to Topsy's behavior she finds out that Topsy has no one who personally cares for her. [. . .] Topsy's change (marked by her tears following Eva's declaration [of love for Topsy]) begins at the moment of Eva's individualizing attention. Topsy's conversion is cemented by Eva's death-bed gift to Topsy of a lock of her hair.

Following Eva's death, Topsy is once again accused of stealing. However, when confronted, it turns out she is hiding a book of Eva's given to her as a gift, one of Eva's curls, and a strip of black crape left over from Eva's funeral. When Topsy fears these items are to be taken from her, she pleads with Ophelia to let her keep them. In their relation to Eva, these almost fetishized elements are linked to the change in Topsy's behavior. [. . .] The objects become the building blocks, for Topsy, of the personalized narrative whose absence so acutely marked her pre-conversion state. The change in Topsy serves to illustrate the difference between an arbitrary collection of cultural elements and a collection informed by a governing narrative. It is, for Stowe, as if Eva's intervention moves Topsy from caricature to character.

Stowe's creation of the character of Topsy involved a similar process. Within Stowe's Topsy there were elements of minstrel stereotypes, the trope of the "wild child," and anxiety about the working class. [. . .] The wild child, separated from her mother and mistreated, was a familiar trope in sentimental fiction. In fact, Stowe's solution for the problem of a wild child, the love of a substitute mother, was by no means unusual. What was unique was Stowe's conflation of the wild child with the slave child. This act of articulation made a particular political use of the wild child trope by literally making slavery responsible for an ongoing concern of white, middle-class America, the motherless child in an economically uncertain world. [. . .]

From **Arthur Riss, "Racial Essentialism and Family Values in Uncle Tom's Cabin,"** American Quarterly, 46 (Dec. 1994): 513–44

In a striking way, Arthur Riss reverses the twenty-first-century sense that racial stereotypes oppress and dehumanize. Rather, Riss argues that Stowe used biological racialism (as opposed to racism) to elevate slaves by portraying them to be naturally and essentially Christian. According to Riss, Stowe showed readers that slavery should be abolished because it violated the positive racial stereotype of Africans as moral receivers of Christ.

[. . .] Until recently, critics who cited Stowe's obvious use of racial stereotypes regularly condemned her as a racist and declared that Stowe's belief in inherent racial characteristics tainted, and perhaps even wholly negated, the sincerity and the value of *Uncle Tom's Cabin*'s manifest antislavery politics. In probably the most scathing attack on the novel's racial stereotypes, J.C. Furnas in *Goodbye to Uncle Tom* argues that Stowe's books in general and Uncle Tom's Cabin in particular are intrinsically "racist propaganda" and that "their effect must always have been to instill or strengthen racist ideas."[1] The stereotype that Furnas most objects to is the notion that the African race is inherently affectionate and peaceful. Such a sentimentalization of the "Negro," according to Furnas, has "sadly clogged the efforts of modern good will" and is responsible for "the wrongheadedness, distortions and wishful thinkings about Negroes . . . that still plague us today." Furnas acknowledges that the popular use of the Uncle Tom epithet "is unfair to the figure that Mrs. Stowe created," but he nevertheless reproves Stowe for having so "persuasively formulated and thus frozen" an "apparently authoritative racist doctrine to plump out" her readers' "previously inchoate notions." As Furnas melodramatically concludes, the "devil could have forged no shrewder weapon for the Negro's worst enemy." [. . .]

[C]ontemporary liberal belief [maintains] that racialism intrinsically supports an oppressive social hierarchy and thus too quickly conflates racialism with racism. [. . .] Historically, this tendency to condemn essentialism axiomatically becomes suspect once Stowe's account of racial essences is situated within an

---

1 J.C. Furnas, *Goodbye to Uncle Tom* (New York, 1956). Furnas's argument expands on the claims made by James Baldwin in "Everybody's Protest Novel" (see **pp. 40–2**).

antebellum context. [. . .] [I]t is Stowe's particular version of racial essentialism that must be recovered. For when it is, it becomes clear that Stowe advocates the abolition of slavery not by discrediting racialism but by advocating a stronger sense of biological racialism. One cannot forget that the most effective way Stowe elicits sympathy for Negroes is by giving them an essentially Christian character. [. . .]

For Stowe, the most significant personal characteristic of Africans is their essential affinity for Christianity. Negroes, as Tom most clearly demonstrates, have "a natural genius for religion"; "in their gentleness, their lowly docility of heart, their aptitude to repose on a superior mind and rest on a higher power, their child-like simplicity of affection and facility of forgiveness . . . they will exhibit the highest form of the peculiarly Christian life." Of "all races of the earth," Stowe repeatedly tells her readers, "none have received the Gospel with such eager docility." Although the Negro's natural love of Christianity could have been attributed to cultural rather than genetic transmission, Stowe very carefully defines this distinctive feature as biological. The "principle of reliance and unquestioning faith," the foundations of Christianity that Stowe represents so vividly in *Uncle Tom's Cabin* as "more a native element" to the African race than any other, she explains in *The Key to Uncle Tom's Cabin* to be an effect of the fact that the African race is "possessed of a nervous system peculiarly susceptible and impressible." Stowe believes that religious faith is essentially sensational, a matter of the heart. Since the African race is the race most open to sensations, Negroes constitutively possess the greatest sensitivity to the Word of God and are naturally great Christians [. . .]

This racialist claim about the African's instinct for Christianity is clearly a powerful strategy to secure white sympathy for the Negro slave. Such "romantic racialism" opposes the charge of biologically based racial inferiority not by denying biologism but by arguing that the biological identity of the African has been misidentified. In claiming that the Negro race is naturally a Christian race, Stowe appeals to her audience's belief that the Negro is a distinct race but then proceeds to define this biological uniqueness in terms of the moral values that her audience already privileges. Rather than repudiating racialism, Stowe seeks to intensify a particular brand of racialism.

Despite Stowe's undisguised racialist claims about the nature of Africans, many critics uncomfortable with notions of racial essences have tried to argue that Stowe ultimately emphasizes nurture rather than nature. Such attempts at a liberal redemption of Stowe's racial stereotypes, however, overlook the fact that such an environmentalist account of African character would undermine her anti-slavery argument. If Stowe maintained that the surroundings wholly constituted a slave's character, Southerners could then invoke her positive characterization of Tom to prove that slavery benefitted the African. A predominantly environmental or social account of the effects of slavery upon the Negro character either would make it extremely difficult for Stowe to present a heroic slave or would require her to de-emphasize the evils of slavery and to acknowledge that slavery can produce virtuous slaves [. . .]

Although Stowe's biological essentialism clearly could not silence Southern claims about the positive influence of slavery, its presence did work to anticipate and counter the logic of nurture over nature that supported many proslavery arguments. [. . .]

Stowe represents the Emersonian struggle against nature as representative of Anglo-Saxon "coldness." For example, Senator Bird betrays a typically Anglo-Saxon love for the transcendental realm of the "coldly and strictly logical" when, discussing the dangers of disobeying the Fugitive Slave Law, he counsels his wife about letting "feelings run away with our judgment." Though Senator Bird eventually abandons his claims for abstract "duty" when he comes face to face with Eliza, an actual fugitive slave, his sympathy reveals not his ability to go against his racial nature but the tension between Anglo-Saxon coldness and the Christian ethic of compassion.

According to Stowe, it is precisely this instinct for cold abstraction that motivates the essential antagonism between the Anglo-Saxon and the African. As Stowe avers in the first sentence of the novel's preface, "Polite and refined society" in the United States has ignored, misunderstood, and degraded the Negro precisely because the Negro is an "exotic race, whose ancestors, born beneath a tropic sun, brought with them, and perpetuated to their descendants, a character . . . essentially unlike the hard and dominant Anglo-Saxon race." This opening gesture immediately signals Stowe's intention of reinterpreting the Anglo-Saxon's hostility toward the Negro as determined by each race's opposing essences rather than by the superiority or inferiority of each race's level of civilization or intellectual ability. [. . .] Since the Anglo-Saxon mistakes his partial racial genius for a universal principle, he is unable to appreciate the native genius of the African. [. . .]

From **Peter Stoneley, "Sentimental Emasculations: *Uncle Tom's Cabin* and *Black Beauty*,"** *Nineteenth-Century Literature*, 54:1 (June 1999): 53–72

In this essay, Peter Stoneley recognizes that some white authors used black characters to represent both docile animal innocence and uncontrollable animal sexuality. Stoneley analyzes Stowe's attraction to and eroticization of the black body and her interest in showing the black body being beaten and defeated into Christian submission.

[. . .] I want to address once more the question of whether women's fictions do indeed encode emasculating designs. [. . .] I ask what implications such designs may have in relation to women owning and projecting desire, especially in relation to the black male body. My argument relates back to the ideology of passionlessness, inasmuch as I see in emasculatory scenarios a rejection of female, as well as of male, desire. In focusing on the black male body, my chosen texts, Harriet Beecher Stowe's *Uncle Tom's Cabin* (1852) and Anna Sewell's *Black*

Beauty (1877), center upon a doubly problematic desire. The result, I argue, is that these novels both facilitate and impede a consuming gaze. In repeated episodes the black male body is exposed, and punished, at the same time: the narrative's "black desires" are enabled and obscured. But why should a discussion of emasculation be complicated by the inclusion of a racial factor? The answer is in part a matter of empirical fact: in both English and American nineteenth-century cultures, gendered preoccupations often occur in relation to those of race. To conceptualize this fact, we might say that race and gender, blackness and desire, are, to borrow Anne McClintock's phrase, "articulated categories"[1] – that is to say, they are categories that are constructed in and through each other; the question of sexual power frequently invokes that of race, and vice versa. [D.H.] Lawrence,[2] and subsequently Leslie A. Fiedler,[3] drew attention to the fact that white men ran away with black men: Huck with Jim, Hawk-eye with Chingachgook, Ishmael with Queequeg.[4] In all cases, the touchstone of intact maleness is the primitive other, whether animal, black, or Indian. [. . .]

To write about blackness, then, was to write about desire. But to write about blackness was also to avoid desire altogether, for the black figure represents both sexual desire and childish innocence. There is the same contradiction as that between "dumb beasts" and "the Beast," between the helpless and the wicked. The African in particular was thought to be governed more by passion than by the intellect. The black body, perceived to be more sexual, was thought to elicit the treacherous carnality that the white man tried to subjugate and of which the white woman was scarcely aware. [. . .]

Blackness calls forth or threatens to desublimate white desire, and a variety of works show white writers moving between the sexual allure of blackness and the need to reaffirm the superiority of white discipline. The two most famous nineteenth-century women writers to deal with black bodies, Harriet Beecher Stowe and Anna Sewell, both show unruly "black desires" being subjugated to white human discipline. Both writers were attracted by the black or animal body, yet the morality of their fiction dictated that these projections of desire be beaten into Christian humility. In spite of the tendency in abolitionist movements to see the racial other as innocent and childlike, this view is prone to become its opposite. For nineteenth-century white women writers, blackness is structured around an instantly recognizable binary of selfless love and selfish passion, and

---

1   [Stoneley's note.] See Anne McClintock, *Imperial Leather: Race, Gender, and Sexuality in the Colonial Contest* (New York, N.Y.: Routledge, 1995), 4.

2   D.H. Lawrence (1885–1930) was a famous British novelist who wrote, among other works, *Sons and Lovers* (1913), *Women in Love* (1917), and *Lady Chatterly's Lover* (1928). His insightful and acerbic *Studies in Classic American Literature* (1923) has influenced generations of readers of U.S. literature.

3   Leslie Fiedler (1917– 2003), an American critic best-known for his controversial work, *Love and Death in the American Novel* (1960), which analyzes unexplored homosexual themes in the work of Twain, Hawthorne, and other writers.

4   The references are to the white boy Huckleberry Finn and the slave Jim in Mark Twain's *Adventures of Huckleberry Finn* (1884), the white scout Natty Bumppo (also known as Hawkeye) and the Mohican Indian Chingachgook in James Fenimore Cooper's *The Last of the Mohicans* (1826), and to the white sailor Ishmael and the Polynesian harpooner Queequeg in Herman Melville's *Moby-Dick* (1851).

the supposedly passionless lady maintains her moral authority by siding with restraint and self-control. Blackness becomes another opportunity to affirm a Christian, maternal love, even if this result seems to the modern reader to be a rather unconvincing "cover story" for the text's secret "black" desire. [. . .]

[Stowe], as author decrees who shall be whipped; the fantasies of exposure, punishment, and transcendence are hers. This problem of narrative power is compounded when Stowe describes a slaveholder at an auction of slaves. She tells of how he inspects the slaves' bodies by feeling them, making them jump, and generally putting them through their paces, as one would a horse. And the spectators comment on the points of each of the lots. [. . .] Yet that same inventorizing eye is repeatedly deployed by Stowe herself as she lovingly assesses her characters' qualities:

> His black hair, fine as floss silk, hung in glossy curls about his round, dimpled face, while a pair of large dark eyes, full of fire and softness, looked out from beneath the rich, long lashes, as he peered curiously into the apartment.

> He was a large, broad-chested, powerfully-made man, of a full glossy black, and a face whose truly African features were characterized by an expression of grave and steady good sense, united with much kindliness and benevolence.

This maternal sensuousness, close and nurturing, makes a claim on both the body and the spirit. We are invited to love that which makes the figure saleable: the penetrably soft, luxury item of an epicene boy, or the doughty, unquestioning strength of a good field hand. In other words, Stowe invites us as readers to desire and to consume the slave body, and her narrative gaze mimics the trade that it deplores. Any sense of complex humanity is abandoned, allowing Stowe and the reader to take up and inhabit this body with its "full glossy black."

Even in its whiter aspect, blackness represented for Stowe the body and its compulsions. [. . .] Eliza's womanliness, her virtual whiteness, and her training under Mrs. Shelby all serve to mitigate her natural or "animal" passion. George, on the other hand, responds with "passion" to the injustices of his position, to the extent that Eliza keeps begging him not to lose control and do something "wicked," a concern that reminds us that he is marked by a residual African wildness. [. . .] George is sufficiently white and beautiful for Stowe's predominantly white readers to identify with, and yet the tinge of racial otherness lends him an exotic glamor. By virtue of his maleness he encapsulates Stowe's deeper ambivalence, in that he is both attractive and repulsive in his blackness, both "passionate" and "wicked."

A less troubling image of blackness is found in Uncle Tom himself. He is very black, and correspondingly cheerful, child-like, and loving; he is either happy or sad, with no finer shades of feeling. His goodness is also defined in his availability for endless service. [. . .] [F]earsome blackness is not developed in Tom's own character: he has been redeemed, and he does not sink back, atavistically, into the sexual morass from which he has come. [. . .]

Stowe's vision of race is deeply ambivalent. Her blacks are "home-loving and affectionate," and yet they are also sexual and may easily relapse into subhuman monsters. They are animal in that they are simple and innocent, and they are animal in the sense of a brutal and self-seeking physicality. In the latter part of the novel, Legree tries to get Tom to abandon his faith, and to acknowledge Legree as his true master. He makes a practice of beating slave women into submitting to his sexual demands, and he uses similarly vicious means to conquer Tom's spirit. Legree's sexual pursuit of his new slave girl, Emmeline, and his demonic pursuit of Tom's soul are constantly interposed. [. . .] [W]e might say that Tom is having his erotic blackness beaten out of him in a scene that is itself eroticized – the bodily "climax" of the novel. Stowe manages to resolve her own desire for and revulsion at the black body by exposing it and killing it at the same time.

With the destruction of his body, Tom is left entirely pure and ready for Heaven. [. . .] Tom's violent death, though deplored, is also celebrated as a victory, as a way of making the nation safe. Stowe is caught in a series of contradictions: she loves the "animal" body – which is to say that she gives careful, lingering descriptions of blackness, and especially of black males – but she disapproves of the disruptive potential of this same body. Although she deplores Legree's domination and violation of Tom's body, her discourse approves of the domination of the body generally. She shows that desire, signified by blackness, must be purged from the American social body if true womanhood and the order of the family are to be saved.

Stowe is thus ensnared in an equivalent of the Madonna–whore syndrome, in that she cannot accommodate sexual appetite with goodness. For Tom to be a hero he must be transformed into an asexual heroine, and, indeed, Tom's gender is resignified. In defining all good blacks as "home-loving and affectionate," Stowe is placing them within the womanly sphere. [. . .] One can easily understand why Elizabeth Ammons describes Tom as "the supreme heroine of the book."[5] But Stowe cannot quite believe that this kind of Christian emasculation is enough. So Tom is killed, and George is returned to Africa.

From **Cynthia Griffin Wolff, " 'Masculinity' in *Uncle Tom's Cabin*,"** *American Quarterly,* 47(4) (Dec. 1995): 595–618

While James Baldwin denounces the passive and weak characterization of Uncle Tom, Cynthia Griffin Wolff here argues that Tom's "benevolent masculinity" conquers Legree through his nonviolent resistance, especially in Chapters 40 and 41 **(pp. 138–44)**. In a revolutionary gesture, Stowe endows Uncle Tom with the most moral and ethical qualities and emphasizes his African features to demonstrate that his ideal manliness does not derive from any white ancestry.

---

5   [Stoneley's note.] Elizabeth Ammons, "Heroines in *Uncle Tom's Cabin*," *American Literature*, 49 (1977): 173.

[. . .] Stowe's strategies took many forms. Sometimes (especially at the beginning of the novel), she catered to her white audience's prejudiced stereotypes. More often, she drew heavily upon her reader's familiarity with (and tolerance of) the conventions of sentimental fiction – exalting the power of women as peace makers and purveyors of moral wisdom. But nowhere was Stowe more cunningly careful than in the construction of her principal male characters (who were the most potentially threatening to an unsympathetic audience); here, she drew self-consciously upon the notions of masculinity that pervaded abolitionist and reformist thinking at mid-century – especially upon those connected to the doctrine of fraternal love – probably because she was deeply sympathetic with them herself. [. . .]

In her hero, Stowe constructed a man whose emotional and moral life is centered not on domination or competition but on the self-conscious, vigorous exercise of communal love – a man who unites the virtues of "kindliness and benevolence" with dignity and a "broad-chested" and "powerfully made" physique. Consistently, then, Tom's "self-sacrifice" is not a manifestation of weakness but a potent and effective enactment of social responsibility. [. . .]

His tactics of nonviolent opposition consistently follow the strategies of passive resistance and prudent behavior that had already been well-developed by black abolitionists who encountered racist antagonism in the free north. Moreover, given the African Americans' particular concern that black men should be able to protect their families in the wake of the Fugitive Slave Act, Stowe takes care to make it clear that Tom's strategies are always ultimately effective in saving his loved ones. Thus, her reader is presented with this paradox: nonviolent behavior may be an even more productive means of offering protection than acts of aggression (which always carry the possibility of wide-spread, random carnage).

Most radical of all, Stowe not only gives vivid life to the arguments of the nonviolent abolitionists who had been inveighing against America's infatuation with bloodshed, she postulates a black man as the exemplary model of this admirable behavior – a black man who is strong hearted enough to save far more people through the heroism of personal sacrifice than might ever have been saved through vicious battle. Moreover, Stowe's pointed emphasis on Tom's unadulterated "blackness" and on his explicitly "African" features prevented any of her readers from imputing his commendable behavior to some admixture of white blood (as whites were readily inclined to do). At the very least, then, this portrayal specifically refuted the mid-nineteenth-century racist claim of the African Americans' intrinsic inferiority to whites in emotional and moral matters; at the most, it might be construed as confirming the sentiments that had been expressed by such black abolitionists as Crummell – that is, a belief in the black man's moral and emotional superiority (Dickens believed Stowe to be making precisely this claim [see his letter, pp. 33–4]).

This careful, political "leverage" in the creation of Tom is not unique. All of the principal males in the novel can be identified almost schematically as illustrations of the moral and emotional success or failure of different constructions of masculinity. Thus if the black man (Tom) is an ideal of fraternal love successfully enacted, the white man (Augustine St. Clare) is a grotesque distortion of that ideal; he is a man who has become feminized in the most ludicrously reductive and ineffectual understanding of the term – a fact that is especially apparent when the introductory description of St. Clare is compared with that of Tom. [. . .]

Tom engages in pragmatic, nonviolent resistance and saves not only his own family but other blacks as well; St. Clare engages in passive, intellectual day-dreaming and saves no one, not even himself.

If Tom and St. Clare are equal and opposite embodiments of moral sentiment and non-violence, George and Legree are similarly balanced enactments of masculinity constructed along the lines of conquest and aggressive competition. Typically, George construes his identity not communally but in terms of domination – a category he elaborates by consistently defining himself by comparison with other men.

> My master! and who made him my master? . . . I'm a man as much as he is. I'm a better man than he is. I know more about business than he does; I am a better manager than he is; I can read better than he can; I can write a better hand, – and I've learned it in spite of him; and now what right has he to make a dray-horse of me? to take me from things I can do, and do better than he can?

By contrast, Legree is the crude, violent, phallic cartoon of such masculinity, with

> a round bullet-head, large light-gray eyes, with . . . shaggy, sandy eyebrows and stiff, wiry, sunburned hair; . . . his large, coarse mouth was distended with tobacco, the juice of which, from time to time, he ejected from him with great decision and explosive force. [p. 133]

Thus is the legitimacy of a "patriarchal" hierarchy dismissed; thus is the authority of mere brute dominance demolished. In this fictional world, "Legree" is eponymous with naked power, and he is vile. [. . .] Tom's death, then, is both a tragic loss and the definitive demonstration of social corruption – slavery's unwillingness to tolerate a resolutely good man who is also a black man.

Within the terms of this narrative, far from being a recommendation of supine passivity, Tom's strategic use of nonviolent resistance affirms several forms of "conquest": his triumph over Legree is more than the triumph of a singularly heroic black man over a savage white and more than the triumph of Christianity over sin. It is the conquest of communal, benevolent masculinity over a definition of gender that is built upon subjugation and aggression. "You've always stood it out agin me," Legree rages at Tom; "now, I'll *conquer ye or kill ye!*" [p. 139]. When Tom dies, Stowe leaves no doubt that Legree and his vicious mode of conquest have been morally and emotionally supplanted.

> "What a thing 't is to be a Christian!" [Tom whispered]. . . . He began to draw his breath with long, deep inspirations, and his broad chest rose

and fell heavily. The expression of his face was that of a *conqueror*. [**p. 143** (emphasis added)]

Stowe's twentieth-century readers may not sympathize with Tom's joy in Christian love. Nonetheless, all can share Stowe's hope that America would discard its imperialistic veneration of revolution, conquest, and brute force – and that it would embrace new ideals to build a more noble Republic.

In this context, the consignment of George Harris and his family to a "happy ending" in Liberia is not so much problematic as it is enigmatic. His talents combine with his name to remind the reader of America's own founding father. The possibility that he might play precisely that role for his own people seems his own most ardent wish. However, are we compelled to believe that he must leave America to enact such a role? Stowe seems to claim as much.

> It is with the oppressed, enslaved African race that I cast in my lot; and, if I wished anything, I would wish myself two shades darker rather than one lighter. The desire and yearning of my soul is for an African *nationality*. I want a people that shall have a tangible, separate existence of its own; and where am I to look for it? Not in Hayti . . . Where, then, shall I look? On the shores of Africa I see a republic. . . . There it is my wish to go, and find myself a people. [**p. 147**]

Black abolitionists were expressing just such expectations as these in antislavery newspapers at the time that Stowe was writing *Uncle Tom's Cabin*; their opinions initiated a mid-nineteenth-century "back to Africa" movement. [. . .] Thus one explanation for Stowe's decision is timely: she is echoing this current pro-African sentiment. Yet, the puzzling fact remains that in this fictional world, George Harris seems to have no "place" – that he must be dispatched "elsewhere." [. . .] Nonetheless, even in her own day, Stowe's decision to banish George was sometimes criticized and was condemned as a revival of the recolonization movement and an expression of racial prejudice.

From **Jean Fagan Yellin, "Doing It Herself:** *Uncle Tom's Cabin* **and Woman's Role in the Slavery Crisis,"** in *New Essays on Uncle Tom's Cabin*, ed. Eric J. Sundquist (New York, N.Y.: Cambridge University Press, 1986)

Pointing out that Stowe divides *Uncle Tom's Cabin* into two groups, Christians and non-Christians, Jean Fagin Yellin notes that the Christians in the novel tend to be white women and slaves and that the non-Christians are mostly white men. Yellin examines the implications of race and gender on Christian values and emphasizes the expansive role Stowe's view of Christian life offered women.

[. . .] *Uncle Tom's Cabin* is primarily a Christian novel; most importantly, it frames the mundane struggle for black emancipation in the United States in the universal spiritual struggle for Christian salvation. In contrast to the slave narratives, which focus on the efforts of *black* people to achieve freedom, Stowe's novel explores the moral dilemma of *white* Americans who must decide how to act in the face of the 1850 Fugitive Slave Law: whether to obey the law and apprehend escaped slaves or to act on their feelings of charity, help the fugitives, and break the law. Repeatedly, the free white individuals faced with these moral dilemmas are women. [. . .]

Eva is (as her mother laments) hopelessly democratic. Always seeming "somehow to put herself on an equality with every creature that comes near her," she embodies an egalitarian Christian love. Her vision undermines the authoritarian religiosity endorsed by Marie's proslavery minister [. . .] But Little Eva's importance rests elsewhere. She lives and dies a divine child. Powerless on earth, powerful in heaven, Stowe's female exemplar is less an advocate of mundane emancipation than a model of heavenly salvation. As her conversion of Topsy demonstrates, she is a spiritual, not a political, liberator. [. . .]

Miss Ophelia seems a more likely candidate than Little Eva for the role of female abolitionist. But as the action unfolds, it becomes clear that Ophelia St. Clare is not representative of the northern women the Grimkés [abolitionist sisters] had recruited into female antislavery societies. [. . .]

Although she deplored slavery, in Vermont Miss Ophelia had not been a member of the local abolitionist society. [. . .] Ophelia's mildest comments enflame Marie's advocacy of slavery, and her debate with St. Clare becomes an occasion for him to echo the denunciatory testimonials of antislavery southerners. [. . .] In *Uncle Tom's Cabin*, slavery is condemned by a southern male, not a northern female; when Miss Ophelia attempts to soften St. Clare's militant male rhetoric, she is vitiating a southerner's attack on slavery. [. . .]

When Miss Ophelia gains legal title to Topsy, she is transformed from a representative "woman of the nominally free states" into a slaveholding "Christian woman of the South." [. . .]

Although Ophelia St. Clare may serve as a model for southern women by Christianizing, educating, and emancipating her slave, and for northern women by overcoming her racism, perhaps Mary Bird is the most important model for Stowe's readers among women of "the nominally free states" whose involvement with slaves and slavery was less intimate. Stowe's dramatization of the invasion of Mrs. Bird's Ohio home by slavery's evil presence demonstrates that slavery shapes not only southern homes like the Shelbys' and the St. Clares' but also northern domestic life [. . .]

Refusing to take seriously her husband's arguments and explanations, Mrs. Bird rests her case [. . .] asserting, "Now, John, I don't know anything about politics, but I can read my Bible; and there I see that I must feed the hungry, clothe the naked, and comfort the desolate; and that Bible I mean to follow" [**p. 91**]. Not satisfied with proclaiming her defiance, she attacks her husband's position until an interruption signals the appearance of the runaway Eliza and her son. It is only after the female fugitive has successfully appealed to the northern woman for protection, only after the free woman and the female fugitive slave have established their sisterhood as bereaved mothers, that the senator suggests a plan for Eliza's escape. [. . .]

Stowe's *Uncle Tom's Cabin* includes a number of nonwhite female characters – slave, fugitive, and free – but although it follows their physical actions with some attention, it expresses little interest in their moral choices. Indeed, in *Uncle Tom's Cabin* neither male nor female nonwhite characters are seriously treated as rational creatures engaged in the human activity of making moral choices, but instead are seen as natural creatures reacting to events. Like all of Stowe's characters, however, they have the duty to be Christians and to help others follow Christ.

Accordingly, Eliza Harris is shown as a Christian wife and mother who influences the spiritual salvation of her husband and children [. . .] [W]hen her little son Harry is threatened, she automatically obeys the voice of nature and attempts his rescue; finally free and safe, after converting her husband to Christianity, she happily follows him to Africa in an effort to save the pagans. [. . .] But we are not shown Eliza agonizing over her decisions; these are presented as simple reactions, not reasoned moral choices. Even Cassy, the prototypical "tragic mulatto" on the Legree place who, maddened by sexual abuse, once killed her baby to save him from a life of slavery, receives similar treatment. Although it is this dark female who tempts Tom to abandon his faith, her abrupt conversion occurs within the space of a single sentence.

Stowe consistently presents her blacker female figures with even less complexity. Although Topsy and Aunt Chloe, the most important ones, are first seen as comic and then shown as Christians, the moral choices inevitably involved in their transformations are scanted. Stowe's serious concern with the morality of free white aristocratic "Christian women of the South" and free white "women of the nominally free states" – women like Emily Shelby, Marie St. Clare, Ophelia St. Clare, Mary Bird and Rachael Halliday – contrasts dramatically with her summary treatment of the moral conflicts of black and mulatto female characters like the hard-working Chloe, the battered child Topsy, the heroic slave mother Eliza, and even the sexually abused Cassy. [. . .]

In *Uncle Tom's Cabin*, none of the characters – black, mulatto or white, male or female – becomes involved in the public struggle against slavery [. . .] The narrator's announcement that her objective is "to awaken sympathy and feeling for the African race, as they exist among us," suggests that sympathy is a force essentially destructive of human injustice. Despite the negative example of Marie St. Clare (who is incapable of sympathizing with anyone), both the action and the narration of the novel demonstrate that women have easy access to this revolutionary power. Yet none of Stowe's female characters uses it [. . .] collectively to challenge institutionalized injustice in the public sphere. Instead, *Uncle Tom's Cabin* shows individual women using the power of sympathy to enable them to act effectively in private against slavery when the servile institution threatens the domestic sphere. Stowe's female Christians act successfully against slavery without walking out of their own front doors.

To the extent that, within the process of defending Christian domestic values,

Stowe's emphasis on individual sympathy and on the doctrine of Higher Laws functions not only as a critique of chattel slavery but also as a critique of racist patriarchal capitalist culture in America, and to the extent that it suggests an alternative society grounded in egalitarian Christianity and proposes a loving maternal ethic in opposition to patriarchal values, *Uncle Tom's Cabin* endorses nineteenth-century radical ideas.

In this regard, the crucial connections between sex and race in *Uncle Tom's Cabin* demand examination. The primary distinctions in Stowe's book are between non-Christians and Christians. Stowe assigns intellectual superiority and worldly power to the first group and spiritual superiority and otherworldly power – seen as infinitely more important – to the second. In the process, she conflates race and sex. Her first group consists primarily of white males. Her second group includes essentially white females and all nonwhites.

The connections between Uncle Tom, the cultural type of the True Woman, and Stowe's view of Jesus Christ have been repeatedly noted. [. . .] Stowe's novel echoes other nineteenth-century analyses, however, in connecting "women and Negroes" not only in terms of their earthly powerlessness, but also as the reservoirs of a sympathy that signals their heavenly power and revolutionary potential. [. . .] At issue here is how Christians should use that power. [. . .]

The Work in Performance

Uncle Tom's Cabin contains great dramatic potential: wild chases and daring escapes, scenes of brutal abuse, numerous character types, tearful reunions, and angelic deathbed scenes. Because mid-century playwrights and entrepreneurs understood the novel's powerful mix of sentiment and high drama, stage versions began appearing immediately. One early theatrical adaptation even premiered in Baltimore in January 1852, before the publication of the novel's last installment in the *National Era* and before the novel's publication in book form.

An actor named George L. Aiken wrote a short play in 1852 that ended with Eva's death, and its success prompted him to script a sequel that ended with Uncle Tom's death. In a strategic move, Aiken combined his two plays to produce a long version that ran for 100 nights before 25,000 spectators, a theatrical record at the time. Aiken's success compelled many entrepreneurs to stage productions, including Phineas T. Barnum, the effervescent American showman, who produced a profitable version. Soon other cities began mounting their own shows, and *Uncle Tom's Cabin* as a theatrical event became an institution called "Tomming." By 1900 over 500 theater troupes were mounting productions.

In these productions, Uncle Tom, Topsy, and other black characters in the novel were played by white actors in blackface, a practice called minstrelsy. With makeup, white minstrel actors darkened their faces, exaggerated the features of their hair, lips, noses, and eyes, and danced in grotesque caricature of African Americans. Blackface minstrelsy began in the 1830s as songs and dances performed in theaters and bars for comic entertainment for white audiences, who believed that what they saw on stage was an accurate portrayal of black speech, movement, and physical appearance. While minstrel shows served as entertainment, they also no doubt provided white audiences the benefit of being able to feel racially superior as they watched degrading stereotypes of African Americans.

Thus, stage productions of *Uncle Tom's Cabin* curiously advocated abolition through a medium based on racial exploitation and misrepresentation. The slur of accusing a black person of being an "Uncle Tom," that is, subservient and submissive to whites, derived not from the novel, but from stage adaptations that blended Uncle Tom with such stock minstrel characters as Jim Crow, after whom racially segregated laws would be named. While the practice of minstrelsy would by today's standards be considered outrageously and intolerably racist, it was considered normal and acceptable by most whites in the early nineteenth century.

Theatrical versions changed many other details of the novel. For example, while Stowe portrays Eliza's perilous escape to freedom across the icy Ohio River as suspenseful and emotionally gratifying, the scene nevertheless is only a paragraph long. On stage, however, Eliza's flight became more detailed and enthralling as packs of bloodhounds pursued her. Simon Legree's lascivious interest in Cassy and Emmeline, intended to rouse censure from the reader, instead provided theater-goers with a spicy touch of lurid stimulation. Also, Eva's role as a holy and pure exemplar of Christian love was exaggerated so that, in some productions, she rose to heaven on wings.

Many white southerners opposed productions of Uncle Tom plays. Susie King Taylor, an African American woman who published a memoir about her life during the Civil War, wrote that an organization of descendants of Confederate soldiers "sent a petition to the managers of the local theatres in Tennessee to prohibit the performance of 'Uncle Tom's Cabin,' claiming it was exaggerated (that is, the treatment of the slaves), and would have a very bad effect on the children who might see the drama."[1] In other words, some white southerners believed that stage versions of *Uncle Tom's Cabin* would unfairly depict slavery as bad and cruel, which would contradict white southern values that upheld the value and necessity of human bondage.

Stowe herself did not endorse the dramatization of her novel, and even though it ran longer than any other play in U.S. history, she did not earn any profits. Stowe distanced herself from the novel's dramatization because many devout Christian families considered the theater an immoral arena. Perhaps because Stowe's father and husband, as preachers, gave dramatic "performances" in their pulpits, they all understood the power of performative language to sway emotion and resolve. At mid-century, theaters were often visited by men and women of loose morals and theater-goers enjoyed drinking alcohol before and during shows. Stowe did not want her highly moral story of slavery to be associated with un-Christian behavior or to lure Christian viewers to the theater and then tempt them to return for other productions and provocations.

Uncle Tom's Cabin even affected the development of the moving picture industry, for an important early silent film was Edwin S. Porter's *Uncle Tom's Cabin* (1903). The novel has been filmed many times since. The first African American Tom was played by Sam Lucas in 1917. Most recently, Stan Lathan directed a version for the cable TV station Showtime in 1987 starring Avery Brooks, Phylicia Rashad, Samuel L. Jackson, Edward Woodward, and Bruce Dern. The novel also plays a fascinating role in Rodgers and Hammerstein's popular musical film *The King and I* (1956), which traces the life of the English governess Mrs. Anna

---

1   Susie King Taylor, *A Black Woman's Civil War Memoirs: Reminiscences of My Life in Camp with the 33rd U.S. Colored Troops, Late 1st South Carolina Volunteers*, ed. Patricia W. Romero (New York, N.Y: Markus Wiener Publishing, 1988), 139.

Leonowens (Deborah Kerr) at the Siamese court of King Mongkut (Yul Brynner). To entertain some important English visitors, members of the royal court perform the "Small House of Uncle Thomas," which doubles as the harem girl Tuptim's (Rita Moreno) plea for freedom.

3

Key Passages

Introduction

Uncle Tom's Cabin cuts back and forth between two stories: one, a story about a slave named Uncle Tom as he is sold further south into slavery, and two, a story about a slave family escaping north to freedom. As readers follow the progress of the characters both north and south, we meet a host of other characters who help Stowe articulate her argument against slavery.

The Key Passages selected below have been chosen in order to maintain coherence of plot and to demonstrate Stowe's brilliant range and complexity of characterization. The story begins in Kentucky, on the Shelby slave plantation. Mr. Shelby, to stave off financial difficulty, agrees to sell two of his slaves: the loyal and religious Uncle Tom and a little boy named Harry. Harry's mother Eliza overhears details of the transaction and warns Uncle Tom to escape, as she plans to with her son. Uncle Tom refuses to escape and instead trusts his fate to God. Eliza grabs her boy and runs, even jumping on shifting sheets of ice to cross the Ohio River from the slave state of Kentucky to the free state of Ohio.

Eliza runs to the home of Senator Bird, who has just voted in favor of the Fugitive Slave Law, which forbids northerners to assist runaway slaves. Eliza's plight challenges his feelings of national duty, and Mrs. Bird's sympathetic appeal on behalf of Eliza and Harry forces the Senator to change his mind. Eliza is also assisted by some Quakers, whose generosity reunites Eliza with her husband.

On a boat heading south, Uncle Tom saves the life of Eva St. Clare, an angelic little girl, who convinces her father to buy the noble slave. Uncle Tom and Eva form a deep bond, and Eva's dying vision of racial equality brings many slaves to Christ. Eva's father, Augustine St. Clare, discusses many ideas about slavery with his northern cousin, Miss Ophelia, who decides to raise and educate a slave, Topsy.

When St. Clare dies, all of his slaves are sold, and Uncle Tom is bought by the evil Simon Legree, who hates the way Uncle Tom assists other slaves. Choosing not to reveal the whereabouts of two escaped slaves, Uncle Tom dies, Christ-like, from the numerous lashes with which Legree punishes him.

The novel ends with a happy vision of many restored family ties and an eloquent appeal to readers to make the correct moral decision.

Key Passages

Preface

In her "Preface" to the novel, Stowe states that her purpose in writing *Uncle Tom's Cabin* is "to awaken sympathy and feeling for the African race." Thus, she clearly establishes a didactic and political purpose to her creative endeavor. We can see many forces at work here in the Preface: moral outrage, abolitionism, sentiment, prevailing racial ideologies (Anglo-Saxons as "hard and dominant," unlike the native African character), and devout Christian belief. See her "Preface" to *A Key to Uncle Tom's Cabin* (**pp. 24–5**).

The scenes of this story, as its title indicates, lie among a race hitherto ignored by the associations of polite and refined society; an exotic race, whose ancestors, born beneath a tropic sun, brought with them, and perpetuated to their descendants, a character so essentially unlike the hard and dominant Anglo-Saxon race, as for many years to have won from it only misunderstanding and contempt.

But, another and better day is dawning; every influence of literature, of poetry and of art, in our times, is becoming more and more in unison with the great master chord of Christianity, "good will to man."

The poet, the painter, and the artist, now seek out and embellish the common and gentler humanities of life, and, under the allurements of fiction, breathe a humanizing and subduing influence, favorable to the development of the great principles of Christian brotherhood.

The hand of benevolence is everywhere stretched out, searching into abuses, righting wrongs, alleviating distresses, and bringing to the knowledge and sympathies of the world the lowly, the oppressed, and the forgotten.

In this general movement, unhappy Africa at last is remembered; Africa, who began the race of civilization and human progress in the dim, gray dawn of early time, but who, for centuries, has lain bound and bleeding at the foot of civilized and Christianized humanity, imploring compassion in vain.

But the heart of the dominant race, who have been her conquerors, her hard masters, has at length been turned towards her in mercy; and it has been seen how far nobler it is in nations to protect the feeble than to oppress them. Thanks be to God, the world has at last outlived the slave-trade!

The object of these sketches is to awaken sympathy and feeling for the African race, as they exist among us; to show their wrongs and sorrows, under a system so necessarily cruel and unjust as to defeat and do away the good effects of all that can be attempted for them, by their best friends, under it.

In doing this, the author can sincerely disclaim any invidious feeling towards those individuals who, often without any fault of their own, are involved in the trials and embarrassments of the legal relations of slavery.

Experience has shown her that some of the noblest of minds and hearts are often thus involved; and no one knows better than they do, that what may be gathered of the evils of slavery from sketches like these, is not the half that could be told, of the unspeakable whole.

In the northern states, these representations may, perhaps, be thought caricatures; in the southern states are witnesses who know their fidelity. What personal knowledge the author has had, of the truth of incidents such as here are related, will appear in its time.

It is a comfort to hope, as so many of the world's sorrows and wrongs have, from age to age, been lived down, so a time shall come when sketches similar to these shall be valuable only as memorials of what has long ceased to be.

When an enlightened and Christianized community shall have, on the shores of Africa, laws, language and literature, drawn from among us, may then the scenes of the house of bondage be to them like the remembrance of Egypt to the Israelite,[1] – a motive of thankfulness to Him who hath redeemed them!

Chapter 1: In Which the Reader is Introduced to a Man of Humanity

The opening chapter introduces the reader to a "man of humanity," Mr. Arthur Shelby, a slave owner who seems kind in contrast to Mr. Haley and others. But "a man of humanity" is also ironic and challenges readers who uphold a belief in benevolent slave masters because Mr. Shelby nonetheless owns other humans and, because he has fallen into debt, has just sold his loyal and devoutly Christian slave, Uncle Tom, as well as a young boy named Harry. This chapter also introduces us to Mr. Shelby's beautiful slave, Eliza, who rightfully suspects that Mr. Shelby has sold her son Harry to get out of debt.

---

1   Stowe draws upon American slaves' common reference, as symbolic of their own plight, to the biblical story of Pharaoh's enslavement of Israelites until Moses led them to freedom.

[. . .] Perhaps the mildest form[1] of the system of slavery is to be seen in the State of Kentucky. The general prevalence of agricultural pursuits of a quiet and gradual nature, not requiring those periodic seasons of hurry and pressure that are called for in the business of more southern districts, makes the task of the negro a more healthful and reasonable one; while the master, content with a more gradual style of acquisition, has not those temptations to hardheartedness which always over-come frail human nature when the prospect of sudden and rapid gain is weighed in the balance, with no heavier counterpoise than the interests of the helpless and unprotected.

Whoever visits some estates there, and witnesses the good humored indulgence of some masters and mistresses, and the affectionate loyalty of some slaves, might be tempted to dream the oft-fabled poetic legend of a patriarchal institution, and all that; but over and above the scene there broods a portentous shadow – the shadow of *law*. So long as the law considers all these human beings, with beating hearts and living affections, only as so many *things* belonging to a master, – so long as the failure, or misfortune, or imprudence, or death of the kindest owner, may cause them any day to exchange a life of kind protection and indulgence for one of hopeless misery and toil, – so long it is impossible to make anything beautiful or desirable in the best regulated administration of slavery.

Mr. Shelby was a fair average kind of man, good-natured and kindly, and disposed to easy indulgence of those around him, and there had never been a lack of anything which might contribute to the physical comfort of the negroes on his estate. He had, however, speculated largely and quite loosely; had involved himself deeply, and his notes to a large amount had come into the hands of Haley [a hard-driving slave trader] [. . .]

Now, it had so happened that, in approaching the door, Eliza had caught enough of the conversation to know that a trader was making offers to her master for somebody.

She would gladly have stopped at the door to listen, as she came out; but her mistress just then calling, she was obliged to hasten away.

Still she thought she heard the trader make an offer for her boy; – could she be mistaken? Her heart swelled and throbbed, and she involuntarily strained him so tight that the little fellow looked up into her face in astonishment.

"Eliza, girl, what ails you to-day?" said her mistress, when Eliza had upset the wash-pitcher, knocked down the work-stand, and finally was abstractedly offering her mistress a long night-gown in place of the silk dress she had ordered her to bring from the wardrobe.

Eliza started. "O, missis!" she said, raising her eyes; then, bursting into tears, she sat down in a chair, and began sobbing.

"Why, Eliza, child! what ails you?" said her mistress.

"O! missis, missis," said Eliza, "there's been a trader talking with master in the parlor! I heard him."

---

1   Historically, slaves tended to regard conditions in Kentucky to be less harsh than slave life further south, such as in Mississippi. Hence, slaves feared being "sold down river" (down the Mississippi River) to the cotton plantations deeper south that required even more back-breaking labor.

"Well, silly child, suppose there has."

"O, missis, *do* you suppose mas'r would sell my Harry?" And the poor creature threw herself into a chair, and sobbed convulsively.

"Sell him! No, you foolish girl! You know your master never deals with those southern traders, and never means to sell any of his servants, as long as they behave well. Why, you silly child, who do you think would want to buy your Harry? Do you think all the world are set on him as you are, you goosie? Come, cheer up, and hook my dress. There now, put my back hair up in that pretty braid you learnt the other day, and don't go listening at doors any more."

"Well, but, missis, *you* never would give your consent – to – to – "

"Nonsense, child! to be sure, I shouldn't. What do you talk so for? I would as soon have one of my own children sold. But really, Eliza, you are getting altogether too proud of that little fellow. A man can't put his nose into the door, but you think he must be coming to buy him."

Reassured by her mistress' confident tone, Eliza proceeded nimbly and adroitly with her toilet, laughing at her own fears, as she proceeded.

Mrs. Shelby was a woman of a high class, both intellectually and morally. To that natural magnanimity and generosity of mind which one often marks as characteristic of the women of Kentucky, she added high moral and religious sensibility and principle, carried out with great energy and ability into practical results. Her husband, who made no professions to any particular religious character, nevertheless reverenced and respected the consistency of hers, and stood, perhaps, a little in awe of her opinion. Certain it was that he gave her unlimited scope in all her benevolent efforts for the comfort, instruction, and improvement of her servants, though he never took any decided part in them himself. In fact, if not exactly a believer in the doctrine of the efficiency of the extra good works of saints, he really seemed somehow or other to fancy that his wife had piety and benevolence enough for two – to indulge a shadowy expectation of getting into heaven through her superabundance of qualities to which he made no particular pretension.

The heaviest load on his mind, after his conversation with the trader, lay in the foreseen necessity of breaking to his wife the arrangement contemplated, – meeting the importunities and opposition which he knew he should have reason to encounter.

Mrs. Shelby, being entirely ignorant of her husband's embarrassments, and knowing only the general kindliness of his temper, had been quite sincere in the entire incredulity with which she had met Eliza's suspicions. In fact, she dismissed the matter from her mind, without a second thought; and being occupied in preparations for an evening visit, it passed out of her thoughts entirely.

Mrs. Shelby is horrified by her husband's business transaction and provides a mother's perspective on the evil of selling children away from parents and on the evil of selling such a divine soul as Uncle Tom. Nonetheless, Mr. Shelby follows through with the deal. Determined to save her child and Uncle Tom, whom Mr. Shelby has sold to the trader Haley, Eliza runs to warn Uncle Tom, who decides not to flee. Eliza has been separated from her husband, George Harris, who was hired out to work in a factory, where he invented a labor-saving machine. George's master, however, fails to appreciate George's ingenuity and instead assigns him menial labor and another woman to be his wife. George desperately wants his freedom and plans to run away to Canada where he hopes to earn money to purchase Eliza and Harry.

Chapter 7: The Mother's Struggle

Chapter 7 includes one of the most famous scenes in American literature – Eliza escaping to freedom by jumping from ice floe to ice floe to cross from the slave state of Kentucky to the free state of Ohio – and one that gripped nineteenth-century theater-going audiences again and again. Stowe taps the power of sentiment by directly asking readers who are mothers how fast they could run if their child were threatened, and she directly compares Eliza's crossing the Ohio River to freedom to Israelites crossing the River Jordan to freedom.

See Frances Harper's poem "Eliza Harris" (p. 22) for a nineteenth-century African American poet's debt to Stowe, and Stowe's letter to Eliza Cabot Follen (pp. 18–20) which links the death of Stowe's baby to slave mothers' loss. In her novel *Beloved*, Toni Morrison sets the scene of Sethe giving birth to Denver at this very same location: the watery border between "states" of bondage and freedom.

It is impossible to conceive of a human creature more wholly desolate and forlorn than Eliza, when she turned her footsteps from Uncle Tom's cabin.

Her husband's suffering and dangers, and the danger of her child, all blended in her mind, with a confused and stunning sense of the risk she was running, in leaving the only home she had ever known, and cutting loose from the protection of a friend whom she loved and revered. Then there was the parting from every familiar object, – the place where she had grown up, the trees under which she had played, the groves where she had walked many an evening in happier days, by the side of her young husband, – everything, as it lay in the clear, frosty starlight, seemed to speak reproachfully to her, and ask her whither could she go from a home like that?

But stronger than all was maternal love, wrought into a paroxysm of frenzy by the near approach of a fearful danger. Her boy was old enough to have walked by her side, and, in an indifferent case, she would only have led him by the hand; but now the bare thought of putting him out of her arms made her shudder, and she strained him to her bosom with a convulsive grasp, as she went rapidly forward.

The frosty ground creaked beneath her feet, and she trembled at the sound;

every quaking leaf and fluttering shadow sent the blood backward to her heart, and quickened her footsteps. She wondered within herself at the strength that seemed to be come upon her; for she felt the weight of her boy as if it had been a feather, and every flutter of fear seemed to increase the supernatural power that bore her on, while from her pale lips burst forth, in frequent ejaculations, the prayer to a Friend above – "Lord, help! Lord, save me!"

If it were *your* Harry, mother, or your Willie, that were going to be torn from you by a brutal trader, to-morrow morning, – if you had seen the man, and heard that the papers were signed and delivered, and you had only from twelve o'clock till morning to make good your escape, – how fast could *you* walk? How many miles could you make in those few brief hours, with the darling at your bosom, – the little sleepy head on your shoulder, – the small, soft arms trustingly holding on to your neck?

For the child slept. At first, the novelty and alarm kept him waking; but his mother so hurriedly repressed every breath or sound, and so assured him that if he were only still she would certainly save him, that he clung quietly round her neck, only asking, as he found himself sinking to sleep,

"Mother, I don't need to keep awake, do I?"

"No, my darling; sleep, if you want to."

"But, mother, if I do get asleep, you won't let him get me?"

"No! so may God help me!" said his mother, with a paler cheek, and a brighter light in her large dark eyes.

"You're *sure*, an't you, mother?"

"Yes, *sure*!" said the mother, in a voice that startled herself; for it seemed to her to come from a spirit within, that was no part of her; and the boy dropped his little weary head on her shoulder, and was soon asleep. How the touch of those warm arms, the gentle breathings that came in her neck, seemed to add fire and spirit to her movements! It seemed to her as if strength poured into her in electric streams, from every gentle touch and movement of the sleeping, confiding child. Sublime is the dominion of the mind over the body, that, for a time, can make flesh and nerve impregnable, and string the sinews like steel, so that the weak become so mighty.

The boundaries of the farm, the grove, the wood-lot, passed by her dizzily, as she walked on; and still she went, leaving one familiar object after another, slacking not, pausing not, till reddening daylight found her many a long mile from all traces of any familiar objects upon the open highway. [. . .]

After a while, they came to a thick patch of woodland, through which murmured a clear brook. As the child complained of hunger and thirst, she climbed over the fence with him; and, sitting down behind a large rock which concealed them from the road, she gave him a breakfast out of her little package. The boy wondered and grieved that she could not eat; and when, putting his arms round her neck, he tried to wedge some of his cake into her mouth, it seemed to her that the rising in her throat would choke her.

"No, no, Harry darling! mother can't eat till you are safe! We must go on – on – till we come to the river!" And she hurried again into the road, and again constrained herself to walk regularly and composedly forward.

She was many miles past any neighborhood where she was personally known. If she should chance to meet any who knew her, she reflected that the well-known kindness of the family would be of itself a blind to suspicion, as making it an unlikely supposition that she could be a fugitive. As she was also so white as not to be known as of colored lineage, without a critical survey, and her child was white also, it was much easier for her to pass on unsuspected. [. . .]

It was now early spring, and the river was swollen and turbulent; great cakes of floating ice were swinging heavily to and fro in the turbid waters. Owing to the peculiar form of the shore on the Kentucky side, the land bending far out into the water, the ice had been lodged and detained in great quantities, and the narrow channel which swept round the bend was full of ice, piled one cake over another, thus forming a temporary barrier to the descending ice, which lodged, and formed a great, undulating raft, filling up the whole river, and extending almost to the Kentucky shore. [. . .]

In consequence of all the various delays, it was about three-quarters of an hour after Eliza had laid her child to sleep in the village tavern that the [search] party came riding into the same place. Eliza was standing by the window, looking out in another direction, when [Mr. Haley's slave] Sam's quick eye caught a glimpse of her. Haley and [Mr. Haley's slave] Andy were two yards behind. At this crisis, Sam contrived to have his hat blown off, and uttered a loud and characteristic ejaculation, which startled her at once; she drew suddenly back; the whole train swept by the window, round to the front door.

A thousand lives seemed to be concentrated in that one moment to Eliza. Her room opened by a side door to the river. She caught her child, and sprang down the steps towards it. The trader caught a full glimpse of her, just as she was disappearing down the bank; and throwing himself from his horse, and calling loudly on Sam and Andy, he was after her like a hound after a deer. In that dizzy moment her feet to her scarce seemed to touch the ground, and a moment brought her to the water's edge. Right on behind they came; and, nerved with strength such as God gives only to the desperate, with one wild cry and flying leap, she vaulted sheer over the turbid current by the shore, on to the raft of ice beyond. It was a desperate leap – impossible to anything but madness and despair; and Haley, Sam, and Andy, instinctively cried out, and lifted up their hands, as she did it.

The huge green fragment of ice on which she alighted pitched and creaked as her weight came on it, but she staid there not a moment. With wild cries and desperate energy she leaped to another and still another cake; – stumbling – leaping – slipping – springing upwards again! Her shoes are gone – her stockings cut from her feet – while blood marked every step; but she saw nothing, felt nothing, till dimly, as in a dream, she saw the Ohio side, and a man helping her up the bank.

"Yer a brave gal, now, whoever ye ar!" said the man with an oath.

Eliza recognized the voice and face of a man who owned a farm not far from her old home.

"O, Mr. Symmes! – save me – do save me – do hide me!" said Eliza.

"Why, what's this?" said the man. "Why, if 'tan't Shelby's gal!"

"My child! – this boy! – he'd sold him! There is his Mas'r," said she, pointing to the Kentucky shore. "O, Mr. Symmes, you've got a little boy!"

"So I have," said the man, as he roughly, but kindly, drew her up the steep bank. "Besides, you're a right brave gal. I like grit, wherever I see it."

When they had gained the top of the bank, the man paused.

"I'd be glad to do something for ye," said he; "but then there's nowhar I could take ye. The best I can do is to tell ye to go *thar*," said he pointing to a large white house which stood by itself, off the main street of the village. "Go thar; they're kind folks. Thar's no kind o' danger but they'll help you, – they're up to all that sort o' thing."

"The Lord bless you!" said Eliza, earnestly.

"No 'casion, no 'casion in the world," said the man. "What I've done's of no 'count."

"And, oh, surely, sir, you won't tell any one!"

"Go to thunder, gal! What do you take a feller for? Of course not," said the man. "Come, now, go along like a likely, sensible gal, as you are. You've arnt your liberty, and you shall have it, for all me."

The woman folded her child to her bosom, and walked firmly and swiftly away. The man stood and looked after her.

"Shelby, now, mebbe won't think this yer the most neighborly thing in the world; but what's a feller to do? If he catches one of my gals in the same fix, he's welcome to pay back. Somehow I never could see no kind o' critter a strivin' and pantin', and trying to clar theirselves, with the dogs arter 'em, and go agin 'em. Besides, I don't see no kind of 'casion for me to be hunter and catcher for other folks, neither."

So spoke this poor, heathenish Kentuckian, who had not been instructed in his constitutional relations,[2] and consequently was betrayed into acting in a sort of Christianized manner, which, if he had been better situated and more enlightened, he would not have been left to do.

Haley had stood a perfectly amazed spectator of the scene, till Eliza had disappeared up the bank [. . .]

Chapter 9: In Which it Appears that a Senator is But a Man

The dangerous ice prevents Mr. Haley from crossing the Ohio River, although the strength of Eliza's love enables her to reach the shore of a free state. Mr. Symmes directs Eliza to the Ohio home of Senator Bird, who has just voted in favour of Ohio passing the Fugitive Slave Act, which prohibits northerners from

---

2   Most likely a reference to a fugitive slave law. Stowe here suggests that U.S. constitutional law stands in direct opposition to Christian law.

aiding escaped slaves. Mrs. Bird, like Mrs. Shelby, proves to be more moral than her husband. This chapter draws heavily on the power of maternal sympathy to move Senator Bird and readers to tears. Thus, Senator Bird's tears prove that he is but a man, and sentiment moves him to violate the very law he supported. See Catherine Beecher's *A Treatise on Domestic Economy* (**pp. 17–18**) for her articulation of women's superior morality, as well as the excerpts from essays by Tompkins (**pp. 42–7**), Lang (**pp. 54–7**), and Yellin (**pp. 71–4**).

The light of the cheerful fire shone on the rug and carpet of a cosey parlor, and glittered on the sides of the tea-cups and well-brightened teapot, as Senator Bird was drawing off his boots, preparatory to inserting his feet in a pair of new handsome slippers, which his wife had been working for him while away on his senatorial tour. Mrs. Bird, looking the very picture of delight, was superintending the arrangements of the table, ever and anon mingling admonitory remarks to a number of frolicsome juveniles, who were effervescing in all those modes of untold gambol and mischief that have astonished mothers ever since the flood. [. . .]

"[A] cup of your good hot tea, and some of our good home living, is what I want. It's a tiresome business, this legislating!"

And the senator smiled, as if he rather liked the idea of considering himself a sacrifice to his country.

"Well," said his wife, after the business of the tea-table was getting rather slack, "and what have they been doing in the Senate?"

Now, it was a very unusual thing for gentle little Mrs. Bird ever to trouble her head with what was going on in the house of the state, very wisely considering that she had enough to do to mind her own. Mr. Bird, therefore, opened his eyes in surprise, and said,

"Not very much of importance."

"Well; but is it true that they have been passing a law forbidding people to give meat and drink to those poor colored folks that come along? I heard they were talking of some such law, but I didn't think any Christian legislature would pass it!"

"Why, Mary, you are getting to be a politician, all at once."

"No, nonsense! I wouldn't give a fip[1] for all your politics, generally, but I think this is something downright cruel and unchristian. I hope, my dear, no such law has been passed."

"There has been a law passed forbidding people to help off the slaves that come over from Kentucky, my dear; so much of that thing has been done by these reckless Abolitionists, that our brethren in Kentucky are very strongly excited, and it seems necessary, and no more than Christian and kind, that something should be done by our state to quiet the excitement."

---

1   A southern colloquialism for a very small amount of money.

"And what is the law? It don't forbid us to shelter these poor creatures a night, does it, and to give 'em something comfortable to eat, and a few old clothes, and send them quietly about their business?"

"Why, yes, my dear; that would be aiding and abetting, you know."

Mrs. Bird was a timid, blushing little woman, of about four feet in height, and with mild blue eyes, and a peach-blow complexion, and the gentlest, sweetest voice in the world; – as for courage, a moderate-sized cock-turkey had been known to put her to rout at the very first gobble, and a stout house-dog, of moderate capacity, would bring her into subjection merely by a show of his teeth. Her husband and children were her entire world, and in these she ruled more by entreaty and persuasion than by command or argument. There was only one thing that was capable of arousing her, and that provocation came in on the side of her unusually gentle and sympathetic nature; – anything in the shape of cruelty would throw her into a passion, which was the more alarming and inexplicable in proportion to the general softness of her nature. Generally the most indulgent and easy to be entreated of all mothers, still her boys had a very reverent remembrance of a most vehement chastisement she once bestowed on them, because she found them leagued with several graceless boys of the neighborhood, stoning a defenceless kitten. [. . .]

On the present occasion, Mrs. Bird rose quickly, with very red cheeks which quite improved her general appearance, and walked up to her husband, with quite a resolute air, and said, in a determined tone,

"Now, John, I want to know if you think such a law as that is right and Christian?"

"You won't shoot me, now, Mary, if I say I do!"

"I never could have thought it of you, John; you didn't vote for it?"

"Even so, my fair politician."

"You ought to be ashamed, John! Poor, homeless, houseless creatures! It's a shameful, wicked, abominable law, and I'll break it, for one, the first time I get a chance; and I hope I *shall* have a chance, I do! Things have got to a pretty pass, if a woman can't give a warm supper and a bed to poor, starving creatures, just because they are slaves, and have been abused and oppressed all their lives, poor things!"

"But, Mary, just listen to me. Your feelings are all quite right, dear, and interesting, and I love you for them; but, then, dear, we mustn't suffer our feelings to run away with our judgment; you must consider it's not a matter of private feeling, – there are great public interests involved, – there is such a state of public agitation rising, that we must put aside our private feelings."

"Now, John, I don't know anything about politics, but I can read my Bible; and there I see that I must feed the hungry, clothe the naked, and comfort the desolate; and that Bible I mean to follow."

"But in cases where your doing so would involve a great public evil – "

"Obeying God never brings on public evils. I know it can't. It's always safest, all round, to *do as He* bids us."

"Now, listen to me, Mary, and I can state to you a very clear argument, to show –"

"O, nonsense, John! you can talk all night, but you wouldn't do it. I put it to you, John, – would *you* now turn away a poor, shivering, hungry creature from your door, because he was a runaway? *Would* you, now?"

Now, if the truth must be told, our senator had the misfortune to be a man who had a particularly humane and accessible nature, and turning away anybody that was in trouble never had been his forte; and what was worse for him in this particular pinch of the argument was, that his wife knew it, and, of course, was making an assault on rather an indefensible point. So he had recourse to the usual means of gaining time for such cases made and provided; he said "ahem," and coughed several times, took out his pocket-handkerchief, and began to wipe his glasses. Mrs. Bird, seeing the defenceless condition of the enemy's territory, had no more conscience than to push her advantage.

"I should like to see you doing that, John – I really should! Turning a woman out of doors in a snow-storm, for instance; or, may be you'd take her up and put her in jail, wouldn't you? You would make a great hand at that!"

"Of course, it would be a very painful duty," began Mr. Bird, in a moderate tone.

"Duty, John! don't use that word! You know it isn't a duty – it can't be a duty! If folks want to keep their slaves from running away, let 'em treat 'em well, – that's my doctrine. If I had slaves (as I hope I never shall have), I'd risk their wanting to run away from me, or you either, John. I tell you folks don't run away when they are happy; and when they do run, poor creatures! they suffer enough with cold and hunger and fear, without everybody's turning against them; and, law or no law, I never will, so help me God!"

"Mary! Mary! My dear, let me reason with you."

"I hate reasoning, John, – especially reasoning on such subjects. There's a way you political folks have of coming round and round a plain right thing; and you don't believe in it yourselves, when it comes to practice. [. . .]"
[. . .]

After a moment, his wife's voice was heard at the door, in a quick earnest tone, – "John! John! I do wish you'd come here, a moment."

He laid down his paper, and went into the kitchen, and started, quite amazed at the sight that presented itself: – A young and slender woman with garments torn and frozen, with one shoe gone, and the stocking torn away from the cut and bleeding foot, was laid back in a deadly swoon upon two chairs. There was the impress of the despised race on her face, yet none could help feeling its mournful and pathetic beauty, while its stony sharpness, its cold, fixed, deathly aspect, struck a solemn chill over him. He drew his breath short, and stood in silence. His wife and their only colored domestic, old Aunt Dinah, were busily engaged in restorative measures; while old Cudjoe had got the boy on his knee and was busy pulling off his shoes and stockings, and chafing his little cold feet. [. . .]

"O, ma'am!" said she, wildly, to Mrs. Bird, "do protect us! don't let them get him!"

"Nobody shall hurt you here, poor woman," said Mrs. Bird, encouragingly. "You are safe; don't be afraid."

"God bless you!" said the woman, covering her face and sobbing; while the little boy, seeing her crying, tried to get into her lap.

With many gentle and womanly offices, which none knew better how to render than Mrs. Bird, the poor woman was, in time, rendered more calm. A temporary bed was provided for her on the settle, near the fire; and, after a short time, she fell into a heavy slumber, with the child, who seemed no less weary, soundly sleeping on her arm; for the mother resisted, with nervous anxiety, the kindest attempts to take him from her; and even in sleep, her arm encircled him with all unrelaxing clasp, as if she could not even then be beguiled of her vigilant hold. [. . .]

"You needn't be afraid of anything; we are friends here, poor woman! Tell me where you came from, and what you want," said [Mrs Bird].

"I came from Kentucky," said the woman.

"When?" said Mr. Bird, taking up the interrogatory.

"To-night."

"How did you come?"

"I crossed on the ice."

"Crossed on the ice!' said every one present.

"Yes," said the woman, slowly, "I did. God helping me, I crossed on the ice; for they were behind me – right behind – and there was no other way!"

"Law, Missis," said [their black servant] Cudjoe, "the ice is all in broken-up blocks, a swinging and a tetering up and down in the water!"

"I know it was – I know it!" said she, wildly; "but I did it! I wouldn't have thought I could, – I didn't think I should get over, but I didn't care! I could but die, if I didn't. The Lord helped me; nobody knows how much the Lord can help 'em, till they try," said the woman, with a flashing eye.

"Were you a slave?" said Mr. Bird.

"Yes, sir; I belonged to a man in Kentucky."

"Was he unkind to you?"

"No, sir; he was a good master."

"And was your mistress unkind to you?"

"No, sir – no! my mistress was always good to me."

"What could induce you to leave a good home, then, and run away and go through such dangers?"

The woman looked up at Mrs. Bird, with a keen, scrutinizing glance, and it did not escape her that she was dressed in deep mourning.

"Ma'am," she said, suddenly, "have you ever lost a child?"

The question was unexpected, and it was a thrust on a new wound; for it was only a month since a darling child of the family had been laid in the grave.

Mr. Bird turned around and walked to the window, and Mrs. Bird burst into tears; but, recovering her voice, she said,

"Why do you ask that? I have lost a little one."

"Then you will feel for me. I have lost two, one after another, – left 'em buried there when I came away; and I had only this one left. I never slept a night without him; he was all I had. He was my comfort and pride, day and night; and, ma'am, they were going to take him away from me, – to *sell* him, – sell him down south, ma'am, to go all alone, – a baby that had never been away from his mother in his life! I couldn't stand it, ma'am. I knew I never should be good for anything, if they did; and when I knew the papers were signed, and he was sold, I took him and came off in the night; and they chased me, – the man that bought him, and some of Mas'r's folks, – and they were coming down right behind me, and I heard 'em. I jumped right on to the ice; and how I got across, I don't know, – but, first I knew, a man was helping me up the bank."

The woman did not sob nor weep. She had gone to a place where tears are dry; but every one around her was, in some way characteristic of themselves, showing signs of hearty sympathy.

The two little boys, after a desperate rummaging in their pockets, in search of those pocket-handkerchiefs which mothers know are never to be found there, had thrown themselves disconsolately into the skirts of their mother's gown, where they were sobbing, and wiping their eyes and noses, to their hearts' content; – Mrs. Bird had her face fairly hidden in her pocket-handkerchief; and old Dinah, with tears streaming down her black, honest face, was ejaculating, "Lord have mercy on us!" with all the fervor of a camp-meeting;[2] – while old Cudjoe, rubbing his eyes very hard with his cuffs, and making a most uncommon variety of wry faces, occasionally responded in the same key, with great fervor. Our senator was a statesman, and of course could not be expected to cry, like other mortals; and so he turned his back to the company, and looked out of the window, and seemed particularly busy in clearing his throat and wiping his spectacle-glasses, occasionally blowing his nose in a manner that was calculated to excite suspicion, had any one been in a state to observe critically.

"How came you to tell me you had a kind master?" he suddenly exclaimed, gulping down very resolutely some kind of rising in his throat, and turning suddenly round upon the woman.

"Because he *was* a kind master; I'll say that of him, any way; – and my mistress was kind; but they couldn't help themselves. They were owing money; and there was some way, I can't tell how, that a man had a hold on them, and they were obliged to give him his will. I listened, and heard him telling mistress that, and she begging and pleading for me, – and he told her he couldn't help himself, and that the papers were all drawn; – and then it was I took him and left my home, and came away. I knew 'twas no use of my trying to live, if they did it; for 't 'pears like this child is all I have."

"Have you no husband?"

"Yes, but he belongs to another man. His master is real hard to him, and won't let him come to see me, hardly ever; and he's grown harder and harder upon us, and he threatens to sell him down south, – it's like I'll never see *him* again!"

The quiet tone in which the woman pronounced these words might have led a superficial observer to think that she was entirely apathetic; but there was a calm, settled depth of anguish in her large, dark eye, that spoke of something far otherwise.

---

2   At religious revival meetings popular in the nineteenth century, worshipers would often reach a
    fevered state of devotion and be moved to tears.

"And where do you mean to go, my poor woman?" said Mrs. Bird.

"To Canada, if I only knew where that was. Is it very far off, is Canada?" said she, looking up, with a simple, confiding air, to Mrs. Bird's face.

"Poor thing!" said Mrs. Bird, involuntarily.

"Is't a very great way off, think?" said the woman, earnestly.

"Much further than you think, poor child!" said Mrs. Bird; "but we will try to think what can be done for you. Here, Dinah, make her up a bed in your own room, close by the kitchen, and I'll think what to do for her in the morning. Meanwhile, never fear, poor woman; put your trust in God; he will protect you."

Mrs. Bird and her husband reentered the parlor. She sat down in her little rocking-chair before the fire, swaying thoughtfully to and fro. Mr. Bird strode up and down the room, grumbling to himself, "Pish! pshaw! confounded awkward business!" At length, striding up to his wife, he said,

"I say, wife, she'll have to get away from here, this very night. [. . .]"

"To-night! How is it possible? – where to?"

"Well, I know pretty well where to," said the senator, beginning to put on his boots, with a reflective air; and, stopping when his leg was half in, he embraced his knee with both hands, and seemed to go off in deep meditation.

"It's a confounded awkward, ugly business," said he, at last, beginning to tug at his boot-straps again, "and that's a fact!" After one boot was fairly on, the senator sat with the other in his hand, profoundly studying the figure of the carpet. "It will have to be done, though, for aught I see, – hang it all!" and he drew the other boot anxiously on, and looked out of the window.

Now, little Mrs. Bird was a discreet woman, – a woman who never in her life said, "I told you so!" and, on the present occasion, though pretty well aware of the shape her husband's meditations were taking, she very prudently forbore to meddle with them, only sat very quietly in her chair, and looked quite ready to hear her liege lord's intentions, when he should think proper to utter them. [. . .]

"Your heart is better than your head, in this case, John," said the wife, laying her little white hand on his. "Could I ever have loved you, had I not known you better than you know yourself?" And the little woman looked so handsome, with the tears sparkling in her eyes, that the senator thought he must be a decidedly clever fellow, to get such a pretty creature into such a passionate admiration of him; and so, what could he do but walk off soberly, to see about the carriage. At the door, however, he stopped a moment, and then coming back, he said, with some hesitation,

"Mary, I don't know how you'd feel about it, but there's that drawer full of things – of – of – poor little Henry's." So saying, he turned quickly on his heel, and shut the door after him.

His wife opened the little bed-room door adjoining her room, and, taking the candle, set it down on the top of a bureau there; then from a small recess she took a key, and put it thoughtfully in the lock of a drawer, and made a sudden pause, while two boys, who, boy like, had followed close on her heels, stood looking, with silent, significant glances, at their mother. And oh! mother that reads this, has there never been in your house a drawer, or a closet, the opening of which has been to you like the opening again of a little grave? Ah! happy mother that you are, if it has not been so.

Mrs. Bird slowly opened the drawer. There were little coats of many a form and pattern, piles of aprons, and rows of small stockings; and even a pair of little shoes, worn and rubbed at the toes, were peeping from the folds of a paper. There was a toy horse and wagon, a top, a ball, – memorials gathered with many a tear and many a heart-break! She sat down by the drawer, and, leaning her head on her hands over it, wept till the tears fell through her fingers into the drawer; then suddenly raising her head, she began, with nervous haste, selecting the plainest and most substantial articles, and gathering them into a bundle.

"Mamma," said one of the boys, gently touching her arm, "are you going to give away *those* things?"

"My dear boys," she said, softly and earnestly, "if our dear, loving little Henry looks down from heaven, he would be glad to have us do this. I could not find it in my heart to give them away to any common person – to anybody that was happy; but I give them to a mother more heart-broken and sorrowful than I am, and I hope God will send his blessings with them!" [. . .]

What a situation, now, for a patriotic senator, that had been all the week before spurring up the legislature of his native state to pass more stringent resolutions against escaping fugitives, their harborers and abettors!

Our good senator in his native state had not been exceeded by any of his brethren at Washington, in the sort of eloquence which has won for them immortal renown! How sublimely he had sat with his hands in his pockets, and scouted all sentimental weakness of those who would put the welfare of a few miserable fugitives before great state interests! [. . .]

He had never thought that a fugitive might be a hapless mother, a defenceless child, – like that one which was now wearing his lost boy's little well-known cap; and so, as our poor senator was not stone or steel, – as he was a man, and a downright noblehearted one, too, – he was, as everybody must see, in a sad case for his patriotism. And you need not exult over him, good brother of the Southern States; for we have some inklings that many of you, under similar circumstances, would not do much better. [. . .]

While Uncle Tom's wife, Aunt Chloe, cooks her husband his last meal at home, Haley comes to take Uncle Tom away in chains.

Chapter 11: In Which Property Gets into an Improper State of Mind

George Harris, having run away from his master, adopts the name Henry Butler and enters a hotel in Kentucky that has a sign offering a reward for his capture. This chapter is important for establishing George's sense of self-worth, to

[. . .] Here the conversation was interrupted by the approach of a small one-horse buggy to the inn. It had a genteel appearance, and a well-dressed, gentlemanly man sat on the seat, with a colored servant driving.

The whole party examined the new comer with the interest with which a set of loafers in a rainy day usually examine every new comer. He was very tall, with a dark, Spanish complexion, fine, expressive black eyes, and close-curling hair, also of a glossy blackness. His well-formed aquiline nose, straight thin lips, and the admirable contour of his finely-formed limbs, impressed the whole company instantly with the idea of something uncommon. He walked easily in among the company, and with a nod indicated to his waiter where to place his trunk, bowed to the company, and, with his hat in his hand, walked up leisurely to the bar, and gave in his name as Henry Butler, Oaklands, Shelby County. Turning, with an indifferent air, he sauntered up to the advertisement, and read it over. [. . .]

Mr. Wilson followed him, as one who walks in his sleep; and they proceeded to a large upper chamber, where a new-made fire was crackling, and various servants flying about, putting finishing touches to the arrangements.

When all was done, and the servants departed, the young man deliberately locked the door, and putting the key in his pocket, faced about, and folding his arms on his bosom, looked Mr. Wilson full in the face.

"George!" said Mr. Wilson.

"Yes, George," said the young man.

"I couldn't have thought it!"

"I am pretty well disguised, I fancy," said the young man, with a smile. "A little walnut bark has made my yellow skin a genteel brown and I've dyed my hair black; so you see I don't answer to the advertisement at all."

"O, George! but this is a dangerous game you are playing. I could not have advised you to it."

"I can do it on my own responsibility," said George, with the same proud smile.

We remark, *en passant*,[1] that George was, by his father's side, of white descent. His mother was one of those unfortunates of her race marked out by personal beauty to be the slave of the passions of her possessor, and the mother of children who may never know a father. From one of the proudest families in Kentucky he had inherited a set of fine European features, and a high, indomitable spirit. From his mother he had received only a slight mulatto tinge, amply compensated by its accompanying rich, dark eye. A slight change in the tint of the skin and the color

---

1 French for "incidentally," or "in passing."

of his hair had metamorphosed him into the Spanish-looking fellow he then appeared; and as gracefulness of movement and gentlemanly manners had always been perfectly natural to him, he found no difficulty in playing the bold part he had adopted – that of a gentleman travelling with his domestic. [. . .]

"Well, George, I s'pose you're running away – leaving your lawful master, George – (I don't wonder at it) – at the same time, I'm sorry, George, – yes, decidedly – I think I must say that, George – it's my duty to tell you so."

"Why are you sorry, sir?" said George, calmly.

"Why, to see you, as it were, setting yourself in opposition to the laws of your country."

"*My* country!" said George, with a strong and bitter emphasis; "what country have I, but the grave, – and I wish to God that I was laid there!"

"Why, George, no – no – it won't do; this way of talking is wicked – unscriptural. George, you've got a hard master – in fact, he is – well he conducts himself reprehensibly – I can't pretend to defend him." [. . .]

"I'm willing to go with the case to [God Almighty], and ask Him if I do wrong to seek my freedom."

"These feelings are quite natural, George," said the good-natured man, blowing his nose. "Yes they're natural, but it is my duty not to encourage 'em in you. Yes, my boy, I'm sorry for you, now; it's a bad case – very bad; but the apostle [Paul] says, 'Let every one abide in the condition in which he is called.'[2] We must all submit to the indications of Providence, George, – don't you see?"

George stood with his head drawn back, his arms folded tightly over his broad breast, and a bitter smile curling his lips.

"I wonder, Mr. Wilson, if the Indians should come and take you a prisoner away from your wife and children, and want to keep you all your life hoeing corn for them, if you'd think it your duty to abide in the condition in which you were called. I rather think that you'd think the first stray horse you could find an indication of Providence – shouldn't you?"

The little old gentleman stared with both eyes at this illustration of the case; but, though not much of a reasoner, he had the sense in which some logicians on this particular subject do not excel, – that of saying nothing, where nothing could be said. So, as he stood carefully stroking his umbrella, and folding and patting down all the creases in it, he proceeded on with his exhortations in a general way.

"You see, George, you know, now, I always have stood your friend; and whatever I've said, I've said for your good. Now, here, it seems to me, you're running an awful risk. You can't hope to carry it out. If you're taken, it will be worse with you than ever; they'll only abuse you, and half kill you, and sell you down river."

"Mr. Wilson, I know all this," said George. "I *do* run a risk, but –" he threw open his overcoat, and showed two pistols and a bowie-knife. "There!" he said, "I'm ready for 'em! Down south I never *will* go. No! if it comes to that, I can earn

---

2   1 Corinthians 7.20.

myself at least six feet of free soil, – the first and last I shall ever own in Kentucky!"

"Why, George, this state of mind is awful; it's getting really desperate, George. I'm concerned. Going to break the laws of your country!"

"My country again! Mr. Wilson, *you* have a country; but what country have I, or any one like me, born of slave mothers? What laws are there for us? We don't make them, – we don't consent to them, – we have nothing to do with them; all they do for us is to crush us, and keep us down. Haven't I heard your Fourth-of-July speeches? Don't you tell us all, once a year, that governments derive their just power from the consent of the governed?[3] Can't a fellow *think*, that hears such things? Can't he put this and that together, and see what it comes to?" [. . .]

"See here, now, Mr. Wilson," said George, coming up and sitting himself determinately down in front of him; "look at me, now. Don't I sit before you, every way, just as much a man as you are? Look at my face, – look at my hands, – look at my body," and the young man drew himself up proudly; "why am I *not* a man,[4] as much as anybody? Well, Mr. Wilson, hear what I can tell you. I had a father – one of your Kentucky gentlemen – who didn't think enough of me to keep me from being sold with his dogs and horses, to satisfy the estate, when he died. I saw my mother put up at sheriff's sale, with her seven children. They were sold before her eyes, one by one, all to different masters; and I was the youngest. She came and kneeled down before old Mas'r, and begged him to buy her with me, that she might have at least one child with her; and he kicked her away with his heavy boot. I saw him do it; and the last that I heard was her moans and screams, when I was tied to his horse's neck, to be carried off to his place." [. . .]

This speech, delivered partly while sitting at the table, and partly walking up and down the room, – delivered with tears, and flashing eyes, and despairing gestures, – was altogether too much for the good-natured old body to whom it was addressed, who had pulled out a great yellow silk pocket-handkerchief, and was mopping up his face with great energy.

Chapter 13: The Quaker Settlement

In Chapter 13, we meet the Quaker household of the Hallidays, who, by assisting Eliza, George, and Harry, willingly engage in an act of civil disobedience thus violating the Fugitive Slave Act. This chapter shows the joys of domesticity as all

---

3   To justify his law-breaking actions, George Harris refers to the Declaration of Independence of the United States (1776) "We hold these truths to be self-evident, that all men are created equal, that they are endowed by their Creator with certain unalienable Rights, that among these are Life, Liberty, and the pursuit of Happiness – That to secure these rights, Governments are instituted among Men, deriving their just powers from the consent of the governed . . ."

4   George's rhetoric alludes to the earliest and most famous anti-slavery image: that of a naked African kneeling in chains surrounded by the motto "Am I Not A Man A And A Brother?" The image was commissioned in 1787 by the Quaker-led Society for Effecting the Abolition of the Slave Trade.

in the Quaker settlement work together to prepare a nourishing, sustaining meal. In granting Rachel Halliday the role of leader of her kitchen and table, Stowe demonstrates the radical, subversive, and egalitarian possibility of women's domestic role: by serving dinner to a black man, Rachel breaks federal law yet also shows the fugitive slave the beauty of religious faith.

Stowe brilliantly juxtaposes the active flight north to freedom of Eliza, George, and little Harry, to the passive journey south, deeper into slave country, of Uncle Tom. While George and Eliza Harris become strong, defiant, self-determining heroes, Uncle Tom's passivity as he is dragged in chains at the behest of whites, later generated controversy among readers and scholars alike. Yet Tom is a superior Christian who follows what he believes is the will of God.

See the essays of Catherine Beecher (**pp. 17–18**), Jane Tompkins (**pp. 42–7**), and Amy Schrager Lang (**pp. 54–7**) for ideas on the power of maternal sympathy to change prevailing ideas.

A quiet scene now rises before us. A large, roomy, neatly-painted kitchen, its yellow floor glossy and smooth, and without a particle of dust; a neat, well-blacked cooking-stove; rows of shining tin, suggestive of unmentionable good things to the appetite; glossy green wood chairs, old and firm; a small flag-bottomed rocking-chair, with a patch-work cushion in it, neatly contrived out of small pieces of different colored woollen goods, and a larger sized one, motherly and old, whose wide arms breathed hospitable invitation, seconded by the solicitation of its feather cushions, – a real comfortable, persuasive old chair, and worth, in the way of holiest, homely enjoyment, a dozen of your plush or brochetelle drawing-room gentry; and in the chair, gently swaying back and forward, her eyes bent on some fine sewing, sat our old friend Eliza. Yes, there she is, paler and thinner than in her Kentucky home, with a world of quiet sorrow lying under the shadow of her long eyelashes, and marking the outline of her gentle mouth! It was plain to see how old and firm the girlish heart was grown under the discipline of heavy sorrow; and when, anon, her large dark eye was raised to follow the gambols of her little Harry, who was sporting, like some tropical butterfly, hither and thither over the floor, she showed a depth of firmness and steady resolve that was never there in her earlier and happier days.

By her side sat a woman with a bright tin pan in her lap, into which she was carefully sorting some dried peaches. She might be fifty-five or sixty; but hers was one of those faces that time seems to touch only to brighten and adorn. The snowy lisse crape cap, made after the strait Quaker pattern, – the plain white muslin handkerchief, lying in placid folds across her bosom, – the drab shawl and dress, – showed at once the community to which she belonged. Her face was round and rosy, with a healthful downy softness, suggestive of a ripe peach. Her hair, partially silvered by age, was parted smoothly back from a high placid forehead, on which time had written no inscription, except peace on earth, good will to men, and beneath shone a large pair of clear, honest, loving brown eyes;

you only needed to look straight into them, to feel that you saw to the bottom of a heart as good and true as ever throbbed in woman's bosom. So much has been said and sung of beautiful young girls, why don't somebody wake up to the beauty of old women? If any want to get up an inspiration under this head, we refer them to our good friend Rachel Halliday, just as she sits there in her little rocking-chair.

It had a turn for quacking and squeaking, – that chair had, – either from having taken cold in early life, or from some asthmatic affection, or perhaps from nervous derangement; but, as she gently swung backward and forward, the chair kept up a kind of subdued "creechy crawchy," that would have been intolerable in any other chair. But old Simeon Halliday often declared it was as good as any music to him, and the children all avowed that they wouldn't miss of hearing mother's chair for anything in the world. For why? for twenty years or more, nothing but loving words and gentle moralities, and motherly loving kindness, had come from that chair, – head-aches and heart-aches innumerable had been cured there, – difficulties spiritual and temporal solved there, – all by one good, loving woman, God bless her! [. . .]

Simeon Halliday, a tall, straight, muscular man, in drab coat and pantaloons, and broad brimmed hat, now entered. [. . .]

"Did thee say thy name was Harris?" said Simeon to Eliza, as he reentered.

Rachel glanced quickly at her husband, as Eliza tremulously answered "yes;" her fears, ever uppermost, suggesting that possibly there might be advertisements out for her.

"Mother!" said Simeon, standing in the porch, and calling Rachel out.

"What does thee want, father?" said Rachel, rubbing her floury hands, as she went into the porch.

"This child's husband is in the settlement, and will be here to-night," said Simeon.

"Now, thee doesn't say that, father?" said Rachel, all her face radiant with joy.

"It's really true. Peter was down yesterday, with the wagon, to the other stand, and there he found an old woman and two men; and one said his name was George Harris; and, from what he told of his history, I am certain who he is. He is a bright, likely fellow, too."

"Shall we tell her now?" said Simeon. [. . .]

"To be sure. Isn't it what we are made for? If I didn't love John and the baby, I should not know how to feel for her. Come, now, do tell her, – do!" and [Ruth] laid her hands persuasively on Rachel's arm. "Take her into thy bed-room, there, and let me fry the chicken while thee does it."

Rachel came out into the kitchen, where Eliza was sewing, and opening the door of a small bedroom, said, gently, "Come in here with me, my daughter; I have news to tell thee."

The blood flushed in Eliza's pale face; she rose, trembling with nervous anxiety, and looked towards her boy.

"No, no," said little Ruth, darting up, and seizing her hands. "Never thee fear; it's good news, Eliza, – go in, go in!" And she gently pushed her to the door, which closed after her; and then, turning round, she caught little Harry in her arms, and began kissing him.

"Thee'll see thy father, little one. Does thee know it? Thy father is coming," she said, over and over again, as the boy looked wonderingly at her.

Meanwhile, within the door, another scene was going on. Rachel Halliday drew Eliza toward her, and said, "The Lord hath had mercy on thee, daughter; thy husband hath escaped from the house of bondage."[1]

The blood flushed to Eliza's cheek in a sudden glow, and went back to her heart with as sudden a rush. She sat down, pale and faint.

"Have courage, child," said Rachel, laying her hand on her head. "He is among friends, who will bring him here to-night."

"To-night!" Eliza repeated, "to-night!" The words lost all meaning to her; her head was dreamy and confused; all was mist for a moment.

When she awoke, she found herself snugly tucked up on the bed, with a blanket over her, and little Ruth rubbing her hands with camphor. She opened her eyes in a state of dreamy, delicious languor, such as one has who has long been bearing a heavy load, and now feels it gone, and would rest. The tension of the nerves, which had never ceased a moment since the first hour of her flight, had given way, and a strange feeling of security and rest came over her; and, as she lay, with her large, dark eyes open, she followed, as in a quiet dream, the motions of those about her. She saw the door open into the other room; saw the supper-table, with its snowy cloth; heard the dreamy murmur of the singing tea-kettle, saw Ruth tripping backward and forward, with plates of cake and saucers of preserves, and ever and anon stopping to put a cake into Harry's hand, or pat his head, or twine his curls round her snowy fingers. She saw the ample, motherly form of Rachel, as she ever and anon came to the bed-side, and smoothed and arranged something about the bed-clothes, and gave a tuck here and there, by way of expressing her good-will; and was conscious of a kind of sunshine beaming down upon her from her large, clear, brown eyes. She saw [. . .] little Harry in a high chair, under the shadow of Rachel's ample wing; there were low murmurs of talk, gentle tinkling of tea-spoons, and musical clatter of cups and saucers, and all mingled in a delightful dream of rest; and Eliza slept, as she had not slept before, since the fearful midnight hour when she had taken her child and fled through the frosty star-light.

She dreamed of a beautiful country, – a land, it seemed to her, of rest, – green shores, pleasant islands, and beautifully glittering water; and there, in a house which kind voices told her was a home, she saw her boy playing, a free and happy child. She heard her husband's footsteps; she felt him coming nearer; his arms were around her, his tears falling on her face, and she awoke! It was no dream. The daylight had long faded; her child lay calmly sleeping by her side; a candle was burning dimly on the stand, and her husband was sobbing by her pillow.

The next morning was a cheerful one at the Quaker house. "Mother" was up betimes, and surrounded by busy girls and boys, whom we had scarce time to

---

1   In making this Old Testament reference to the Israelites leaving Egypt, Rachel Halliday suggests that God has protected Eliza and her family and that their escape is part of God's will.

introduce to our readers yesterday, and who all moved obediently to Rachel's gentle "Thee had better," or more gentle "Hadn't thee better?" in the work of getting breakfast; for a breakfast in the luxurious valleys of Indiana is a thing complicated and multiform, and, like picking up the rose-leaves and trimming the bushes in Paradise, asking other hands than those of the original mother. While, therefore, John ran to the spring for fresh water, and Simeon the second sifted meal for corn-cakes, and Mary ground coffee, Rachel moved gently and quietly about, making biscuits, cutting up chicken, and diffusing a sort of sunny radiance over the whole proceeding generally. If there was any danger of friction or collision from the ill-regulated zeal of so many young operators, her gentle "Come! come!" or "I wouldn't, now," was quite sufficient to allay the difficulty. Bards have written of the cestus of Venus,[2] that turned the heads of all the world in successive generations. We had rather, for our part, have the cestus of Rachel Halliday, that kept heads from being turned, and made everything go on harmoniously. We think it is more suited to our modern days, decidedly.

While all other preparations were going on, Simeon the elder stood in his shirt-sleeves before a little looking-glass in the corner, engaged in the anti-patriarchal operation of shaving. Everything went on so sociably, so quietly, so harmoni-ously, in the great kitchen, – it seemed so pleasant to every one to do just what they were doing, there was such an atmosphere of mutual confidence and good fellowship everywhere, – even the knives and forks had a social clatter as they went on to the table; and the chicken and ham had a cheerful and joyous fizzle in the pan, as if they rather enjoyed being cooked than otherwise; – and when George and Eliza and little Harry came out, they met such a hearty, rejoicing welcome, no wonder it seemed to them like a dream. [. . .]

Rachel never looked so truly and benignly happy as at the head of her table. There was so much motherliness and full-heartedness even in the way she passed a plate of cakes or poured a cup of coffee, that it seemed to put a spirit into the food and drink she offered.

It was the first time that ever George had sat down on equal terms at any white man's table; and he sat down, at first, with some constraint and awkwardness; but they all exhaled and went off like fog, in the genial morning rays of this simple, overflowing kindness.

This, indeed, was a home, – *home*, – a word that George had never yet known meaning for; and a belief in God, and trust in his providence, began to encircle his heart, as, with a golden cloud of protection and confidence, dark, misanthropic, pining, atheistic doubts, and fierce despair, melted away before the light of a living Gospel, breathed in living faces, preached by a thousand unconscious acts of love and good will, which, like the cup of cold water given in the name of a disciple, shall never lose their reward.

"Father, what if thee should get found out again?" said Simeon second, as he buttered his cake.

"I should pay my fine," said Simeon, quietly.

2   Stowe recasts Venus, the Roman goddess of beauty and love, as a matronly American religious woman. A "cestus" is a woman's belt.

"But what if they put thee in prison?"

"Couldn't thee and mother manage the farm?" said Simeon, smiling.

"Mother can do almost everything," said the boy. "But isn't it a shame to make such laws?"

"Thee mustn't speak evil of thy rulers, Simeon," said his father, gravely. "The Lord only gives us our worldly goods that we may do justice and mercy; if our rulers require a price of us for it, we must deliver it up."

"Well, I hate those old slaveholders!" said the boy, who felt as unchristian as became any modern reformer.

"I am surprised at thee, son," said Simeon; "thy mother never taught thee so. I would do even the same for the slaveholder as for the slave, if the Lord brought him to my door in affliction."

Simeon second blushed scarlet; but his mother only smiled, and said, "Simeon is my good boy; he will grow older, by and by, and then he will be like his father."

"I hope, my good sir, that you are not exposed to any difficulty on our account," said George, anxiously.

"Fear nothing, George, for therefore are we sent into the world. If we would not meet trouble for a good cause, we were not worthy of our name."

"But, for *me*," said George, "I could not bear it."

"Fear not, then, friend George; it is not for thee, but for God and man, we do it," said Simeon. "And now thou must lie by quietly this day, and to-night, at ten o'clock, Phineas Fletcher will carry thee onward to the next stand, – thee and the rest of thy company. The pursuers are hard after thee; we must not delay."

"If that is the case, why wait till evening?" said George.

"Thou art safe here by daylight, for every one in the settlement is a Friend, and all are watching. It has been found safer to travel by night."

Chapter 14: Evangeline

While sailing down the Mississippi River to be resold in New Orleans, Uncle Tom befriends Evangeline St. Clare, an angelic little girl, and daughter of Augustine St. Clare. When Eva falls overboard, Uncle Tom dives in the water to rescue her. Eva insists that her father buy Uncle Tom. In showing the friendship between Uncle Tom and Little Eva, Stowe seems to suggest simultaneously that children are born without prejudice and that blacks are childlike and innocent. But we should also keep in mind Stowe's goal of advocating emancipation on the grounds that slavery inhibits the development of Christian virtues.

[. . .] What other river [besides the Mississippi] of the world bears on its bosom to the ocean the wealth and enterprise of such another country? – a country whose products embrace all between the tropics and the poles! Those turbid waters [of the Mississippi], hurrying, foaming, tearing along, an apt resemblance of that headlong tide of business which is poured along its wave by a race more vehement and energetic than any the old world ever saw. Ah! would that they did not also bear along a more fearful freight, – the tears of the oppressed, the sighs of the helpless, the bitter prayers of poor, ignorant hearts to an unknown God – unknown, unseen and silent [. . .]

The slanting light of the setting sun quivers on the sea-like expanse of the river; the shivery canes, and the tall, dark cypress, hung with wreaths of dark, funereal moss, glow in the golden ray, as the heavily-laden steamboat marches onward. [. . .]

Among the passengers on the boat was a young gentleman of fortune and family, resident in New Orleans, who bore the name of St. Clare. He had with him a daughter between five and six years of age, together with a lady who seemed to claim relationship to both, and to have the little one especially under her charge.

Tom had often caught glimpses of this little girl, – for she was one of those busy, tripping creatures, that can be no more contained in one place than a sunbeam or a summer breeze, – nor was she one that, once seen, could be easily forgotten.

Her form was the perfection of childish beauty, without its usual chubbiness and squareness of outline. There was about it an undulating and aerial grace, such as one might dream of for some mythic and allegorical being. Her face was remarkable less for its perfect beauty of feature than for a singular and dreamy earnestness of expression, which made the ideal start when they looked at her, and by which the dullest and most literal were impressed, without exactly knowing why. The shape of her head and the turn of her neck and bust was peculiarly noble, and the long golden-brown hair that floated like a cloud around it, the deep spiritual gravity of her violet blue eyes, shaded by heavy fringes of golden brown, – all marked her out from other children and made every one turn and look after her, as she glided hither and thither on the boat. Nevertheless, the little one was not what you would have called either a grave child or a sad one. On the contrary, an airy and innocent playfulness seemed to flicker like the shadow of summer leaves over her childish face, and around her buoyant figure. She was always in motion, always with a half smile on her rosy mouth, flying hither and thither with an undulating and cloud-like tread, singing to herself as she moved as in a happy dream. Her father and female guardian were incessantly busy in pursuit of her, – but, when caught, she melted from them again like a summer cloud; and as no word of chiding or reproof ever fell on her ear for whatever she chose to do, she pursued her own way all over the boat. Always dressed in white, she seemed to move like a shadow through all sorts of places, without contracting spot or stain; and there was not a corner or nook, above or below, where those fairy footsteps had not glided, and that visionary golden head, with its deep blue eyes, fleeted along. [. . .]

Tom, who had the soft, impressible nature of his kindly race, ever yearning toward the simple and childlike, watched the little creature with daily increasing interest. To him she seemed something almost divine; and whenever her golden head and deep blue eyes peered out upon him from behind some dusky cotton-bale, or looked down upon him over some ridge of packages, he half believed that he saw one of the angels stepped out of his New Testament. [. . .]

"What's little missy's name?" said Tom, at last, when he thought matters were ripe to push such an inquiry.

"Evangeline St. Clare," said the little one, "though papa and everybody else call me Eva. Now, what's your name?"

"My name's Tom, the little chil'en used to call me Uncle Tom, way back thar in Kentuck."

"Then I mean to call you Uncle Tom, because, you see, I like you," said Eva. "So, Uncle Tom, where are you going?"

"I don't know, Miss Eva."

"Don't know?" said Eva.

"No. I am going to be sold to somebody. I don't know who."

"My papa can buy you," said Eva, quickly; "and if he buys you, you will have good times. I mean to ask him to, this very day."

"Thank you, my little lady," said Tom.

The boat here stopped at a small landing to take in wood, and Eva, hearing her father's voice, bounded nimbly away. Tom rose up, and went forward to offer his service in wooding, and was soon busy among the hands. [. . .]

Tom was standing just under her on the lower deck, as she fell. He saw her strike the water, and sink, and was after her in a moment. A broad-chested, strong-armed fellow, it was nothing for him to keep afloat in the water, till, in a moment or two, the child rose to the surface, and he caught her in his arms, and, swimming with her to the boat-side, handed her up, all dripping, to the grasp of hundreds of hands, which, as if they had all belonged to one man, were stretched eagerly out to receive her. A few moments more, and her father bore her, dripping and senseless, to the ladies' cabin, where, as is usual in cases of the kind, there ensued a very well-meaning and kind-hearted strife among the female occupants generally, as to who should do the most things to make a disturbance, and to hinder her recovery in every way possible. [. . .]

"Papa, do buy him! it's no matter what you pay," whispered Eva, softly, getting up on a package, and putting her arm around her father's neck. "You have money enough, I know, I want him."

"What for, pussy? Are you going to use him for a rattle-box, or a rocking-horse, or what?"

"I want to make him happy."

"An original reason, certainly." [. . .]

"All right," said Haley, his face beaming with delight; and pulling out an old inkhorn, he proceeded to fill out a bill of sale, which, in a few moments, he handed to the young man.

"I wonder, now, if I was divided up and inventoried," said the latter [Augustine St. Clare], as he ran over the paper, "how much I might bring. Say so much for the shape of my head, so much for a high forehead, so much for arms, and hands, and legs, and then so much for education, learning, talent, honesty, religion! Bless me! there would be small charge on that last, I'm thinking. But come, Eva," he said;

and taking the hand of his daughter, he stepped across the boat, and carelessly putting the tip of his finger under Tom's chin, said good-humoredly, "Look up, Tom, and see how you like your new master."

Tom looked up. It was not in nature to look into that gay, young, handsome face, without a feeling of pleasure; and Tom felt the tears start in his eyes as he said, heartily, "God bless you, Mas'r!"

"Well, I hope he will. What's your name? Tom? Quite as likely to do it for your asking as mine, from all accounts. Can you drive horses, Tom?"

"I've been allays used to horses," said Tom. "Mas'r Shelby raised heaps on 'em."

"Well, I think I shall put you in coachy, on condition that you won't be drunk more than once a week, unless in cases of emergency, Tom."

Tom looked surprised, and rather hurt, and said, "I never drink, Mas'r."

"I've heard that story before, Tom; but then we'll see. It will be a special accommodation to all concerned, if you don't. Never mind, my boy," he added, good-humoredly, seeing Tom still looked grave; "I don't doubt you mean to do well."

"I sartin do, Mas'r," said Tom.

"And you shall have good times," said Eva. "Papa is very good to everybody, only he always will laugh at them."

Chapter 16: Tom's mistress and her opinions

Chapters 16 and 18 develop Stowe's antislavery argument through conversations between Uncle Tom's new master, the lazy but well-meaning Augustine St. Clare; St. Clare's hypochondriac wife Marie, who seems to suffer innumerable vague ills; and St. Clare's practical northern cousin, Miss Ophelia, who has traveled south to help St. Clare take care of Eva (since Eva's mother Marie is constantly indisposed). The idealized Eva and Uncle Tom take delight in each other's company, further infantilizing Uncle Tom but elevating the virtue and innocence of both characters and radically suggesting that a white girl and a black man can be spiritual equals.

[. . .] "O! St. Clare, when will you learn how to treat your servants? It's abominable, the way you indulge them!" said Marie.

"Why, after all, what's the harm of the poor dog's wanting to be like his master; and if I haven't brought him up any better than to find his chief good in cologne and cambric handkerchiefs, why shouldn't I give them to him?"

"And why haven't you brought him up better?" said Miss Ophelia with blunt determination.

"Too much trouble, – laziness, cousin, laziness, – which ruins more souls than you can shake a stick at. If it weren't for laziness, I should have been a perfect angel, myself. I'm inclined to think that laziness is what your old Dr. Botherem, up in Vermont, used to call the 'essence of moral evil.' It's an awful consideration, certainly."

"I think you slaveholders have an awful responsibility upon you," said Miss Ophelia. "I wouldn't have it, for a thousand worlds. You ought to educate your slaves, and treat them like reasonable creatures, – like immortal creatures, that you've got to stand before the bar of God with. That's my mind," said the good lady, breaking suddenly out with a tide of zeal that had been gaining strength in her mind all the morning.

"O! come, come," said St. Clare, getting up quickly; "what do you know about us?" [. . .]

"For my part, I don't see any use in such sort of talk " said Marie. "I'm sure, if anybody does more for servants than we do, I'd like to know who; and it don't do 'em a bit good, – not a particle, – they get worse and worse. As to talking to them, or anything like that, I'm sure I have talked till I was tired and hoarse, telling them their duty, and all that and I'm sure they can go to church when they like, though they don't understand a word of the sermon, more than so many pigs, – so it isn't of any great use for them to go, as I see; but they do go, and so they have every chance; but, as I said before, they are a degraded race, and always will be, and there isn't any help for them; you can't make anything of them, if you try. You see, Cousin Ophelia, I've tried, and you haven't; I was born and bred among them, and I know." [. . .]

A gay laugh from the court rang through the silken curtains of the verandah. St. Clare stepped out, and lifting up the curtain, laughed too.

"What is it?" said Miss Ophelia, coming to the railing.

There sat Tom, on a little mossy seat in the court, every one of his button-holes stuck full of cape jessamines, and Eva, gayly laughing, was hanging a wreath of roses round his neck; and then she sat down on his knee, like a chip-sparrow, still laughing.

"O, Tom you look so funny!"

Tom had a sober, benevolent smile, and seemed, in his quiet way, to be enjoying the fun quite as much as his little mistress. He lifted his eyes, when he saw his master, with a half-deprecating, apologetic air.

"How can you let her? said Miss Ophelia.

"Why not?" said St. Clare.

"Why, I don't know, it seems so dreadful!"

"You would think no harm in a child's caressing a large dog, even if he was black; but a creature that can think, and reason, and feel, and is immortal, you shudder at; confess it, cousin. I know the feeling among some of you northerners well enough. Not that there is a particle of virtue in our not having it; but custom with us does what Christianity ought to do, – obliterates the feeling of personal prejudice. I have often noticed, in my travels north, how much stronger this was with you than with us. You loathe them as you would a snake or a toad, yet you are indignant at their wrongs. You would not have them abused; but you don't want to have anything to do with them yourselves. You would send them to Africa, out of your sight and smell, and then send a missionary or two to do up all the self-denial of elevating them compendiously. Isn't that it?"

"Well, cousin," said Miss Ophelia, thoughtfully, "there may be some truth in this."

"What would the poor and lowly do, without children?" said St. Clare, leaning on the railing, and watching Eva, as she tripped off, leading Tom with her. "Your little child is your only true democrat. Tom, now, is a hero to Eva; his stories are wonders in her eyes, his songs and Methodist hymns are better than an opera, and the traps and little bits of trash in his pocket a mine of jewels, and he the most wonderful Tom that ever wore a black skin. This is one of the roses of Eden that the Lord has dropped down expressly for the poor and lowly, who get few enough of any other kind." [. . .]

If ever Africa shall show an elevated and cultivated race, – and come it must, some time, her turn to figure in the great drama of human improvement, – life will awake there with a gorgeousness and splendor of which our cold western tribes faintly have conceived. In that far-off mystic land of gold, and gems, and spices, and waving palms, and wondrous flowers, and miraculous fertility, will awake new forms of art, new styles of splendor; and the negro race, no longer despised and trodden down, will, perhaps, show forth some of the latest and most magnificent revelations of human life. Certainly they will, in their gentleness, their lowly docility of heart, their aptitude to repose on a superior mind and rest on a higher power, their childlike simplicity of affection, and facility of forgiveness. In all these they will exhibit the highest form of the peculiarly *Christian life*, and, perhaps, as God chasteneth whom he loveth, he hath chosen poor Africa in the furnace of affliction, to make her the highest and noblest in that kingdom which he will set up, when every other kingdom has been tried, and failed; for the first shall be last, and the last first.

The scenes of conversation in the St. Clare household are juxtaposed to the story of George, Eliza, and Harry running north. Haley's hired slave catcher, Tom Loker, shoots at George, who defends himself by shooting back and injuring Loker. Loker's henchmen flee, deserting Loker. Eliza takes pity on Loker and insists he be aided. The slaves' kindness convinces Loker to abandon his old pro-slavery ways.

Chapter 18: Miss Ophelia's Experiences and Opinions

Stowe continues her comparison of North and South by portraying Miss Ophelia, the representative of the North, as being horrified by southern housekeeping methods. As a northerner from the "practical" state of Vermont, Miss Ophelia values order and cleanliness. To her, Marie's and Dinah's slovenly kitchen suggests moral laxity. Although this is a humorous chapter, Stowe's point is that domestic disorder reflects moral disorder. For comments on kitchens, see the essay by Gillian Brown (**pp. 48–51**).

[. . .] Trusted to an unlimited extent by a careless master, who handed him a bill without looking at it, and pocketed the change without counting it, Tom had every facility and temptation to dishonesty; and nothing but an impregnable simplicity of nature, strengthened by Christian faith, could have kept him from it. But, to that nature, the very unbounded trust reposed in him was bond and seal for the most scrupulous accuracy. [. . .]

But, all this time, who shall detail the tribulations manifold of our friend Miss Ophelia, who had begun the labors of a Southern housekeeper?

There is all the difference in the world in the servants of Southern establishments, according to the character and capacity of the mistresses who have brought them up.

South as well as north, there are women who have an extraordinary talent for command, and tact in educating. Such are enabled, with apparent ease, and without severity, to subject to their will, and bring into harmonious and systematic order, the various members of their small estate, – to regulate their peculiarities, and so balance and compensate the deficiencies of one by the excess of another, as to produce a harmonious and orderly system.

Such a housekeeper was Mrs. Shelby, whom we have already described; and such our readers may remember to have met with. If they are not common at the South, it is because they are not common in the world. They are to be found there as often as anywhere; and, when existing, find in that peculiar state of society a brilliant opportunity to exhibit their domestic talent.

Such a housekeeper Marie St. Clare was not, nor her mother before her. Indolent and childish, unsystematic and improvident, it was not to be expected that servants trained under her care should not be so likewise; and she had very justly described to Miss Ophelia the state of confusion she would find in the family, though she had not ascribed it to the proper cause.

The first morning of her regency, Miss Ophelia was up at four o'clock; and having attended to all the adjustments of her own chamber, as she had done ever since she came there, to the great amazement of the chamber-maid, she prepared for a vigorous onslaught on the cupboards and closets of the establishment of which she had the keys.

The store-room, the linen-presses, the china-closet, the kitchen and cellar, that day, all went under an awful review. Hidden things of darkness were brought to light to an extent that alarmed all the principalities and powers of kitchen and chamber, and caused many wonderings and murmurings about "dese yer northern ladies" from the domestic cabinet.

Old Dinah, the head cook, and principal of all rule and authority in the kitchen department, was filled with wrath at what she considered an invasion of privilege. [. . .]

Dinah was a character in her own way, and it would be injustice to her memory not to give the reader a little idea of her. She was a native and essential cook, as much as [Uncle Tom's wife] Aunt Chloe, – cooking being an indigenous talent of the African race; but Chloe was a trained and methodical one, who moved in an orderly domestic harness, while Dinah was a self-taught genius, and, like geniuses in general, was positive, opinionated and erratic, to the last degree.

Like a certain class of modern philosophers, Dinah perfectly scorned logic and reason in every shape, and always took refuge in intuitive certainty; and here she was perfectly impregnable. No possible amount of talent, or authority, or explanation, could ever make her believe that any other way was better than her own, or that the course she had pursued in the smallest matter could be in the least modified. [. . .]

But it was very seldom that there was any failure in Dinah's last results. Though her mode of doing everything was peculiarly meandering and circuitous, and without any sort of calculation as to time and place, – though her kitchen generally looked as if it had been arranged by a hurricane blowing through it, and she had about as many places for each cooking utensil as there were days in the year, – yet, if one would have patience to wait her own good time, up would come her dinner in perfect order, and in a style of preparation with which an epicure could find no fault. [. . .]

Miss Ophelia, after passing on her reformatory tour through all the other parts of the establishment, now entered the kitchen. Dinah had heard, from various sources, what was going on, and resolved to stand on defensive and conservative ground, – mentally determined to oppose and ignore every new measure, without any actual and observable contest. [. . .]

When Miss Ophelia entered the kitchen, Dinah did not rise, but smoked on in sublime tranquility, regarding her movements obliquely out of the corner of her eye, but apparently intent only on the operations around her.

Miss Ophelia commenced opening a set of drawers.

"What is this drawer for, Dinah?" she said.

"It's handy for most anything, Missis," said Dinah. So it appeared to be. From the variety it contained, Miss Ophelia pulled out first a fine damask table-cloth stained with blood, having evidently been used to envelop some raw meat.

"What's this, Dinah? You don't wrap up meat in your mistress' best table-cloths?"

"O Lor, Missis, no; the towels was all a missin', – so I jest did it. I laid out to wash that ar, – that's why I put it thar."

"Shif'less!" said Miss Ophelia to herself, proceeding to tumble over the drawer, where she found a nutmeg-grater and two or three nutmegs, a Methodist hymn-book, a couple of soiled Madras handkerchiefs, some yarn and knitting-work, a paper of tobacco and a pipe, a few crackers, one or two gilded china-saucers with some pomade in them, one or two thin old shoes, a piece of flannel carefully pinned up enclosing some small white onions. [. . .]

In despair, [Miss Ophelia] one day appealed to St. Clare.

"There is no such thing as getting anything like system in this family!"

"To be sure, there isn't," said St. Clare.

"Such shiftless management, such waste, such confusion, I never saw!"

"I dare say you didn't."

"You would not take it so coolly, if you were housekeeper."

"My dear cousin, you may as well understand, once for all, that we masters are divided into two classes, oppressors and oppressed. We who are good-natured and hate severity make up our minds to a good deal of inconvenience. If we *will keep* a shambling, loose, untaught set in the community, for our convenience, why, we must take the consequence. Some rare cases I have seen, of persons, who, by a peculiar tact, can produce order and system without severity; but I'm not one of them, – and so I made up my mind, long ago, to let things go just as they do. I will not have the poor devils thrashed and cut to pieces, and they know it, – and, of course, they know the staff is in their own hands."

"But to have no time, no place, no order, – all going on in this shiftless way!"

"My dear Vermont, you natives up by the North Pole set an extravagant value on time! What on earth is the use of time to a fellow who has twice as much of it as he knows what to do with? As to order and system, where there is nothing to be done but to lounge on the sofa and read, an hour sooner or later in breakfast or dinner isn't of much account. Now, there's Dinah gets you a capital dinner, – soup, ragout, roast fowl, dessert, ice-creams and all, – and she creates it all out of chaos and old night down there, in that kitchen. I think it really sublime, the way she manages. But, Heaven bless us! if we are to go down there, and view all the smoking and squatting about, and hurryscurryation of the preparatory process, we should never eat more! My good cousin, absolve yourself from that! It's more than a Catholic penance, and does no more good. You'll only lose your own temper, and utterly confound Dinah. Let her go her own way."

Chapter 20: Topsy

St. Clare buys the slave girl Topsy as a challenge to his northern cousin, Miss Ophelia, to educate as a missionary would. Northern readers identify with Miss Ophelia's position and understand that love, not just a sense of duty, is needed to help slaves become Christians. For critical commentary on Chapter 20, see essays by Brown (**pp. 48–51**), and O'Loughlin (**p. 60**).

One morning, while Miss Ophelia was busy in some of her domestic cares, St. Clare's voice was heard, calling her at the foot of the stairs.

"Come down here, Cousin; I've something to show you."

"What is it?" said Miss Ophelia, coming down, with her sewing in her hand.

"I've made a purchase for your department, – see here," said St. Clare; and, with the word, he pulled along a little negro girl, about eight or nine years of age.

She was one of the blackest of her race; and her round, shining eyes, glittering as glass beads, moved with quick and restless glances over everything in the room. Her mouth, half open with astonishment at the wonders of the new Mas'r's parlor, displayed a white and brilliant set of teeth. Her woolly hair was braided in sundry little tails, which stuck out in every direction. The expression of her face was an odd mixture of shrewdness and cunning, over which was oddly drawn, like a kind of veil, an expression of the most doleful gravity and solemnity. She was dressed in a single filthy, ragged garment, made of bagging; and stood with her hands demurely folded before her. Altogether, there was something odd and goblin-like about her appearance, – something, as Miss Ophelia afterwards said, "so heathenish," as to inspire that good lady with utter dismay; and, turning to St. Clare, she said,

"Augustine, what in the world have you brought that thing here for?"

"For you to educate, to be sure, and train in the way she should go. I thought she was rather a funny specimen in the Jim Crow line.[1] Here, Topsy," he added, giving a whistle, as a man would to call the attention of a dog, "give us a song, now, and show us some of your dancing."

The black, glassy eyes glittered with a kind of wicked drollery, and the thing struck up, in a clear shrill voice, an odd negro melody, to which she kept time with her hands and feet, spinning round, clapping her hands, knocking her knees together, in a wild, fantastic sort of time, and producing in her throat all those odd guttural sounds which distinguish the native music of her race; and finally, turning a summerset or two, and giving a prolonged closing note, as odd and unearthly as that of a steam-whistle, she came suddenly down on the carpet, and stood with her hands folded, and a most sanctimonious expression of meekness and solemnity over her face, only broken by the cunning glances which she shot askance from the corners of her eyes.

Miss Ophelia stood silent, perfectly paralyzed with amazement.

St. Clare, like a mischievous fellow as he was, appeared to enjoy her astonishment; and, addressing the child again, said,

"Topsy, this is your new mistress. I'm going to give you up to her; see now that you behave yourself."

"Yes, Mas'r," said Topsy, with sanctimonious gravity, her wicked eyes twinkling as she spoke.

"You're going to be good, Topsy, you understand," said St. Clare.

"O yes, Mas'r," said Topsy, with another twinkle, her hands still devoutly folded.

"Now, Augustine, what upon earth is this for?" said Miss Ophelia. "Your house is so full of these little plagues, now, that a body can't set down their foot without treading on 'em. I get up in the morning, and find one asleep behind the door, and see one black head poking out from under the table, one lying on the door-mat, – and they are mopping and mowing and grinning between all the railings, and tumbling over the kitchen floor! What on earth did you want to bring this one for?"

"For you to educate – didn't I tell you? You're always preaching about

---

1 The name Jim Crow, which comes from a character in a popular minstrel song, refers derogatorily to blacks. In U.S. history, Jim Crow statutes were enacted in the South beginning in the 1880s to legalize the already present segregation between blacks and whites.

educating. I thought I would make you a present of a fresh-caught specimen, and let you try your hand on her, and bring her up in the way she should go."

"*I* don't want her, I am sure; – I have more to do with 'em now than I want to."

"That's you Christians, all over! – you'll get up a society, and get some poor missionary to spend all his days among just such heathen. But let me see one of you that would take one into your house with you, and take the labor of their conversion on yourselves! No, when it comes to that, they are dirty and disagreeable, and it's too much care, and so on."

"Augustine, you know I didn't think of it in that light," said Miss Ophelia, evidently softening. "Well, it might be a real missionary work," said she, looking rather more favorably on the child.

St. Clare had touched the right string. Miss Ophelia's conscientiousness was ever on the alert. "But," she added, "I really didn't see the need of buying this one; – there are enough now, in your house, to take all my time and skill."

"Well, then, Cousin," said St. Clare, drawing her aside; "I ought to beg your pardon for my good-for-nothing speeches. You are so good, after all, that there's no sense in them. Why, the fact is, this concern belonged to a couple of drunken creatures that keep a low restaurant that I have to pass by every day, and I was tired of hearing her screaming, and them beating and swearing at her. She looked bright and funny too, as if something might be made of her, – so I bought her, and I'll give her to you. Try, now, and give her a good orthodox New England bringing up,[2] and see what it'll make of her. You know I haven't any gift that way; but I'd like you to try."

"Well, I'll do what I can," said Miss Ophelia; and she approached her new subject very much as a person might be supposed to approach a black spider, supposing them to have benevolent designs toward it.

"She's dreadfully dirty, and half naked," she said.

"Well, take her down stairs, and make some of them clean and clothe her up."

Miss Ophelia carried her to the kitchen regions. [. . .]

It is not for ears polite to hear the particulars of the first toilet of a neglected, abused child. In fact, in this world, multitudes must live and die in a state that it would be too great a shock to the nerves of their fellow-mortals even to hear described. Miss Ophelia had a good, strong, practical deal of resolution; and she went through all the disgusting details with heroic thoroughness, though, it must be confessed, with no very gracious air, – for endurance was the utmost to which her principles could bring her. When she saw, on the back and shoulders of the child, great welts and calloused spots, ineffaceable marks of the system under which she had grown up thus far, her heart became pitiful within her. [. . .]

When arrayed at last in a suit of decent and whole clothing, her hair cropped short to her head, Miss Ophelia, with some satisfaction, said she looked more Christian-like than she did, and in her own mind began to mature some plans for her instruction.

---

2   A Protestant religious education expected of prominent families in and around Boston.

Sitting down before her, she began to question her.

"How old are you, Topsy?"

"Dun no, Missis," said the image, with a grin that showed all her teeth.

"Don't know how old you are? Didn't anybody ever tell you? Who was your mother?"

"Never had none!" said the child, with another grin.

"Never had any mother? What do you mean? Where were you born?"

"Never was born!" persisted Topsy, with another grin, that looked so goblin-like, that, if Miss Ophelia had been at all nervous, she might have fancied that she had got hold of some sooty gnome from the land of Diablerie;[3] but Miss Ophelia was not nervous, but plain and businesslike, and she said, with some sternness,

"You mustn't answer me in that way, child; I'm not playing with you. Tell me where you were born, and who your father and mother were."

"Never was born," reiterated the creature, more emphatically; "never had no father nor mother, nor nothin'. I was raised by a speculator, with lots of others. Old Aunt Sue used to take car on us." [. . .]

"Have you ever heard anything about God, Topsy?"

The child looked bewildered, but grinned as usual.

"Do you know who made you?"

"Nobody, as I knows on," said the child, with a short laugh.

The idea appeared to amuse her considerably; for her eyes twinkled, and she added,

"I spect I grow'd. Don't think nobody never made me."

"Do you know how to sew?" said Miss Ophelia, who thought she would turn her inquiries to something more tangible.

"No, Missis."

"What can you do? – what did you do for your master and mistress?"

"Fetch water, and wash dishes, and rub knives, and wait on folks."

"Were they good to you?"

"Spect they was," said the child, scanning Miss Ophelia cunningly.

Miss Ophelia rose from this encouraging colloquy; St. Clare was leaning over the back of her chair.

"You find virgin soil there, Cousin; put in your own ideas, – you won't find many to pull up."

Miss Ophelia's ideas of education, like all her other ideas, were very set and definite; and of the kind that prevailed in New England a century ago, and which are still preserved in some very retired and unsophisticated parts, where there are no railroads. As nearly as could be expressed, they could be comprised in very few words: to teach them to mind when they were spoken to; to teach them the catechism, sewing, and reading; and to whip them if they told lies. And though, of course, in the flood of light that is now poured on education, these are left far away in the rear, yet it is an undisputed fact that our grandmothers raised some tolerably fair

3 Hell.

men and women under this regime, as many of us can remember and testify. At all events, Miss Ophelia knew of nothing else to do; and, therefore, applied her mind to her heathen with the best diligence she could command.

The child was announced and considered in the family as Miss Ophelia's girl; and, as she was looked upon with no gracious eye in the kitchen, Miss Ophelia resolved to confine her sphere of operation and instruction chiefly to her own chamber. With a self-sacrifice which some of our readers will appreciate, she resolved, instead of comfortably making her own bed, sweeping and dusting her own chamber, – which she had hitherto done, in utter scorn of all offers of help from the chambermaid of the establishment, – to condemn herself to the martyrdom of instructing Topsy to perform these operations, – ah, woe the day! Did any of our readers ever do the same, they will appreciate the amount of her self-sacrifice.

Miss Ophelia began with Topsy by taking her into her chamber, the first morning, and solemnly commencing a course of instruction in the art and mystery of bed-making.

Behold, then, Topsy, washed and shorn of all the little braided tails wherein her heart had delighted, arrayed in a clean gown, with well-starched apron, standing reverently before Miss Ophelia, with an expression of solemnity well befitting a funeral.

"Now, Topsy, I'm going to show you just how my bed is to be made. I am very particular about my bed. You must learn exactly how to do it."

"Yes, ma'am," says Topsy, with a deep sigh, and a face of woful earnestness.

"Now, Topsy, look here, – this is the hem of the sheet, – this is the right side of the sheet, and this is the wrong; – will you remember?"

"Yes, ma'am," says Topsy, with another sigh.

"Well, now, the under sheet you must bring over the bolster, – so, – and tuck it clear down under the mattress nice and smooth, – so, – do you see?"

"Yes, ma'am," said Topsy, with profound attention.

"But the upper sheet," said Miss Ophelia, "must be brought down in this way, and tucked under firm and smooth at the foot, – so, – the narrow hem at the foot."

"Yes, ma'am," said Topsy, as before; – but we will add, what Miss Ophelia did not see, that, during the time when the good lady's back was turned, in the zeal of her manipulations, the young disciple had contrived to snatch a pair of gloves and a ribbon, which she had adroitly slipped into her sleeves, and stood with her hands dutifully folded, as before.

"Now, Topsy, let's see *you* do this," said Miss Ophelia, pulling off the clothes, and seating herself.

Topsy, with great gravity and adroitness, went through the exercise completely to Miss Ophelia's satisfaction; smoothing the sheets, patting out every wrinkle, and exhibiting, through the whole process, a gravity and seriousness with which her instructress was greatly edified. By an unlucky slip, however, a fluttering fragment of the ribbon hung out of one of her sleeves, just as she was finishing, and caught Miss Ophelia's attention. Instantly she pounced upon it. "What's this? You naughty, wicked child, – you've been stealing this!"

The ribbon was pulled out of Topsy's own sleeve, yet was she not in the least disconcerted; she only looked at it with an air of the most surprised and unconscious innocence.

"Laws! why, that ar's Miss Feely's ribbon, an't it? How could it a got caught in my sleeve?"

"Topsy, you naughty girl, don't you tell me a lie, – you stole that ribbon!"

"Missis, I declar for 't, I didn't; – never seed it till dis yer blessed minnit."

"Topsy," said Miss Ophelia, "don't you know it's wicked to tell lies?"

"I never tells no lies, Miss Feely," said Topsy, with virtuous gravity; "it's jist the truth I've been a tellin now, and an't nothin else."

"Topsy, I shall have to whip you, if you tell lies so."

"Laws, Missis, if you's to whip all day, couldn't say no other way," said Topsy, beginning to blubber. "I never seed dat ar, – it must a got caught in my sleeve. Miss Feely must have left it on the bed, and it got caught in the clothes, and so got in my sleeve."

Miss Ophelia was so indignant at the barefaced lie, that she caught the child and shook her.

"Don't you tell me that again!"

The shake brought the gloves on to the floor, from the other sleeve.

"There, you!" said Miss Ophelia, "will you tell me now, you didn't steal the ribbon?"

Topsy now confessed to the gloves, but still persisted in denying the ribbon.

"Now, Topsy," said Miss Ophelia, "if you'll confess all about it, I won't whip you this time." Thus adjured, Topsy confessed to the ribbon and gloves, with woful protestations of penitence.

"Well, now, tell me. I know you must have taken other things since you have been in the house, for I let you run about all day yesterday. Now, tell me if you took anything, and I shan't whip you."

"Laws, Missis! I took Miss Eva's red thing she wars on her neck."

"You did, you naughty child! – Well, what else?"

"I took Rosa's yer-rings, – them red ones."

"Go bring them to me this minute, both of 'em."

"Laws, Missis! I can't, – they's burnt up!"

"Burnt up! – what a story! Go get 'em, or I'll whip you."

Topsy, with loud protestations, and tears, and groans, declared that she *could* not. "They's burnt up, – they was."

"What did you burn 'em up for?" said Miss Ophelia.

"Cause I's wicked, – I is. I's mighty wicked, any how. I can't help it."

Just at this moment, Eva came innocently into the room, with the identical coral necklace on her neck.

"Why, Eva, where did you get your necklace?" said Miss Ophelia.

"Get it? Why, I've had it on all day," said Eva.

"Did you have it on yesterday?"

"Yes; and what is funny, Aunty, I had it on all night. I forgot to take it off when I went to bed."

Miss Ophelia looked perfectly bewildered; the more so, as Rosa, at that instant, came into the room, with a basket of newly-ironed linen poised on her head, and the coral ear-drops shaking in her ears!

"I'm sure I can't tell anything what to do with such a child!" she said, in despair. "What in the world did you tell me you took those things for, Topsy?"

"Why, Missis said I must 'fess; and I couldn't think of nothin' else to 'fess," said Topsy, rubbing her eyes.

"But, of course, I didn't want you to confess things you didn't do," said Miss Ophelia; "that's telling a lie, just as much as the other."

"Laws, now, is it?" said Topsy, with an air of innocent wonder.

"La, there an't any such thing as truth in that limb," said Rosa, looking indignantly at Topsy. "If I was Mas'r St. Clare, I'd whip her till the blood run. I would, – I'd let her catch it!"

"No, no, Rosa," said Eva, with an air of command, which the child could assume at times; "you mustn't talk so, Rosa. I can't bear to hear it."

"La sakes! Miss Eva, you's so good, you don't know nothing how to get along with niggers. There's no way but to cut 'em well up, I tell ye."

"Rosa!" said Eva, "hush! Don't you say another word of that sort!" and the eye of the child flashed, and her cheek deepened its color.

Rosa was cowed in a moment.

"Miss Eva has got the St. Clare blood in her, that's plain. She can speak, for all the world, just like her papa," she said, as she passed out of the room.

Eva stood looking at Topsy.

There stood the two children, representatives of the two extremes of society. The fair, high-bred child, with her golden head, her deep eyes, her spiritual, noble brow, and prince-like movements; and her black, keen, subtle, cringing, yet acute neighbor. They stood the representatives of their races. The Saxon, born of ages of cultivation, command, education, physical and moral eminence; the Afric, born of ages of oppression, submission, ignorance, toil, and vice!

Something, perhaps, of such thoughts struggled through Eva's mind. But a child's thoughts are rather dim, undefined instincts; and in Eva's noble nature many such were yearning and working, for which she had no power of utterance. When Miss Ophelia expatiated on Topsy's naughty, wicked conduct, the child looked perplexed and sorrowful, but said, sweetly,

"Poor Topsy, why need you steal? You're going to be taken good care of, now. I'm sure I'd rather give you anything of mine, than have you steal it."

It was the first word of kindness the child had ever heard in her life; and the sweet tone and manner struck strangely on the wild, rude heart, and a sparkle of something like a tear shone in the keen, round, glittering eye; but it was followed by the short laugh and habitual grin. No! the ear that has never heard anything but abuse is strangely incredulous of anything so heavenly as kindness; and Topsy only thought Eva's speech something funny and inexplicable, – she did not believe it.

But what was to be done with Topsy? Miss Ophelia found the case a puzzler; her rules for bringing up didn't seem to apply. She thought she would take time to think of it; and, by the way of gaining time, and in hopes of some indefinite moral virtues supposed to be inherent in dark closets, Miss Ophelia shut Topsy up in one till she had arranged her ideas further on the subject.

"I don't see," said Miss Ophelia to St. Clare, "how I'm going to manage that child, without whipping her."

"Well, whip her, then, to your heart's content; I'll give you full power to do what you like."

"Children always have to be whipped," said Miss Ophelia; "I never heard of bringing them up without." [. . .]

[Topsy] learned her letters as if by magic, and was very soon able to read plain reading; but the sewing was a more difficult matter. The creature was as lithe as a cat and as active as a monkey, and the confinement of sewing was her abomination; so she broke her needles, threw them slyly out of windows, or down in chinks of the walls; she tangled, broke, and dirtied her thread, or, with a sly movement, would throw a spool away altogether. Her motions were almost as quick as those of a practiced conjurer, and her command of her face quite as great; and though Miss Ophelia could not help feeling that so many accidents could not possibly happen in succession, yet she could not, without a watchfulness which would leave her no time for anything else, detect her. [. . .]

Miss Ophelia busied herself very earnestly on Sundays, teaching Topsy the catechism. Topsy had an uncommon verbal memory, and committed with a fluency that greatly encouraged her instructress.

"What good do you expect it is going to do her?" said St. Clare.

"Why, it always has done children good. It's what children always have to learn, you know," said Miss Ophelia.

"Understand it or not," said St. Clare.

"O, children never understand it at the time; but, after they are grown up, it'll come to them." [. . .]

Topsy, who had stood like a black statue during this discussion, with hands decently folded, now, at a signal from Miss Ophelia, went on:

"Our first parents, being left to the freedom of their own will, fell from the state wherein they were created."

Topsy's eyes twinkled, and she looked inquiringly.

"What is it, Topsy?" said Miss Ophelia.

"Please, Missis, was dat ar state Kintuck?"[4]

"What state, Topsy?"

"Dat state dey fell out of. I used to hear Mas'r tell how we came down from Kintuck."

St. Clare laughed.

"You'll have to give her a meaning, or she'll make one," said he. "There seems to be a theory of emigration suggested there."

"O! Augustine, be still," said Miss Ophelia; "how can I do anything, if you will be laughing?"

"Well, I won't disturb the exercises again, on my honor;" and St. Clare took his

4   Kentucky.

paper into the parlor, and sat down, till Topsy had finished her recitations. They were all very well, only that now and then she would oddly transpose some important words, and persist in the mistake, in spite of every effort to the contrary; and St. Clare, after all his promises of goodness, took a wicked pleasure in these mistakes, calling Topsy to him whenever he had a mind to amuse himself, and getting her to repeat the offending passages, in spite of Miss Ophelia's remonstrances.

"How do you think I can do anything with the child, if you will go on so, Augustine?" she would say.

"Well, it is too bad, – I won't again; but I do like to hear the droll little image stumble over those big words!"

"But you confirm her in the wrong way."

"What's the odds? One word is as good as another to her."

"You wanted me to bring her up right; and you ought to remember she is a reasonable creature, and be careful of your influence over her."

"O, dismal! so I ought; but, as Topsy herself says, 'I's so wicked!'"

In very much this way Topsy's training proceeded, for a year or two, – Miss Ophelia worrying herself, from day to day, with her, as a kind of chronic plague [. . .]

> In Kentucky, Mrs. Shelby and Aunt Chloe work together to devise ways to earn money with which to buy Uncle Tom back. St. Clare's twin brother, Alfred, comes to visit the St. Clares with his son Henrique. Eva teaches her cousin Henrique about treating slaves with love, while Augustine and Alfred St. Clare discuss their need for, yet unease with, the slave system. Little Eva's health begins to decline precipitously.

Chapter 25: The Little Evangelist

> In Chapter 25, Eva showers Topsy with the salvific power of love that she had urged Henrique to show to his slave. Eva's unconditional love brings about a change in Topsy.

[. . .] "What makes you behave so?" said St. Clare, who could not help being amused with the child's expression.

"Spects it's my wicked heart," said Topsy, demurely; "Miss Feely says so."

"Don't you see how much Miss Ophelia has done for you? She says she has done everything she can think of."

"Lor, yes, Mas'r! old Missis used to say so, too. She whipped me a heap harder, and used to pull my har, and knock my head agin the door; but it didn't do me no good! I spects, if they's to pull every spear o' har out of my head, it wouldn't do no good, neither, – I's so wicked! Laws! I's nothin but a nigger, no ways!"

"Well, I shall have to give her up," said Miss Ophelia; "I can't have that trouble any longer."

"Well, I'd just like to ask one question," said St. Clare.

"What is it?"

"Why, if your Gospel is not strong enough to save one heathen child, that you can have at home here, all to yourself, what's the use of sending one or two poor missionaries off with it among thousands of just such? I suppose this child is about a fair sample of what thousands of your heathen are."

Miss Ophelia did not make an immediate answer; and Eva, who had stood a silent spectator of the scene thus far, made a silent sign to Topsy to follow her. There was a little glass-room at the corner of the verandah, which St. Clare used as a sort of reading-room; and Eva and Topsy disappeared into this place.

"What's Eva going about, now?" said St. Clare; "I mean to see."

And, advancing on tiptoe, he lifted up a curtain that covered the glass-door, and looked in. In a moment, laying his finger on his lips, he made a silent gesture to Miss Ophelia to come and look. There sat the two children on the floor, with their side faces towards them. Topsy, with her usual air of careless drollery and unconcern; but, opposite to her, Eva, her whole face fervent with feeling, and tears in her large eyes.

"What does make you so bad, Topsy? Why won't you try and be good? Don't you love *anybody*, Topsy?"

"Donno nothing 'bout love; I loves candy and sich, that's all," said Topsy.

"But you love your father and mother?"

"Never had none, ye know. I telled ye that, Miss Eva."

"O, I know," said Eva, sadly; "but hadn't you any brother, or sister, or aunt, or –"

"No, none on 'em, – never had nothing nor nobody."

"But, Topsy, if you'd only try to be good, you might –"

"Couldn't never be nothin' but a nigger, if I was ever so good," said Topsy. "If I could be skinned, and come white, I'd try then."

"But people can love you, if you are black, Topsy. Miss Ophelia would love you, if you were good."

Topsy gave the short, blunt laugh that was her common mode of expressing incredulity.

"Don't you think so?" said Eva.

"No; she can't bar me, 'cause I'm a nigger! – she'd 's soon have a toad touch her! There can't nobody love niggers, and niggers can't do nothin'! *I* don't care," said Topsy, beginning to whistle.

"O, Topsy, poor child, I love you!" said Eva, with a sudden burst of feeling, and laying her little thin, white hand on Topsy's shoulder; "I love you, because you haven't had any father, or mother, or friends, – because you've been a poor, abused child! I love you, and I want you to be good. I am very unwell, Topsy, and I think I shan't live a great while and it really grieves me, to have you be so naughty. I wish you would try to be good, for my sake; – it's only a little while I shall be with you."

The round, keen eyes of the black child were overcast with tears, – large, bright drops rolled heavily down, one by one, and fell on the little white hand. Yes, in that moment, a ray of real belief, a ray of heavenly love, had penetrated the darkness of her heathen soul! She laid her head down between her knees, and wept and sobbed, – while the beautiful child, bending over her, looked like the picture of some bright angel stooping to reclaim a sinner.

"Poor Topsy!" said Eva, "don't you know that Jesus loves all alike? He is just as willing to love you, as me. He loves you just as I do, – only more, because he is better. He will help you to be good; and you can go to Heaven at last, and be an angel forever, just as much as if you were white. Only think of it, Topsy! – *you* can be one of those spirits bright, Uncle Tom sings about."

"O, dear Miss Eva, dear Miss Eva!" said the child; "I will try, I will try; I never did care nothin' about it before."

St. Clare, at this instant, dropped the curtain. "It puts me in mind of mother," he said to Miss Ophelia. "It is true what she told me; if we want to give sight to the blind, we must be willing to do as Christ did, – call them to us, and *put our hands on them*."

"I've always had a prejudice against negroes," said Miss Ophelia, "and it's a fact, I never could bear to have that child touch me; but, I didn't think she knew it."

"Trust any child to find that out," said St. Clare; "there's no keeping it from them. But I believe that all the trying in the world to better a child, and all the substantial favors you can do them, will never excite one emotion of gratitude, while that feeling of repugnance remains in the heart; – it's a queer kind of a fact, – but so it is."

"I don't know how I can help it," said Miss Ophelia; "they are disagreeable to me, – this child in particular, – how can I help feeling so?"

"Eva does, it seems."

"Well, she's so loving! After all, though, she's no more than Christ-like," said Miss Ophelia; "I wish I were like her. She might teach me a lesson."

"It wouldn't be the first time a little child had been used to instruct an old disciple, if it *were* so," said St. Clare.

Chapter 26: Death

The deathbed scene of Eva has been criticized by many readers for being excessively maudlin, sentimental, and melodramatic. But as she dies, Eva brings many slaves to a commitment to God and the Christian way of life; thus, the innocent, pure Eva becomes a Christ-like figure. The essays by both Lang (**pp. 54–7**) and Tompkins (**pp. 42–7**) address Eva's ability to convert others through her death. Frances Harper's poem "Eva's Farewell" (**p. 23**) shows that Stowe's novel proved fertile ground for the imagination of an important nineteenth-century black poet.

[. . .] The deceitful strength which had buoyed Eva up for a little while was fast passing away; seldom and more seldom her light footstep was heard in the verandah, and oftener and oftener she was found reclined on a little lounge by the open window, her large, deep eyes fixed on the rising and falling waters of the lake. [. . .]

"Mamma, you believe, don't you, that Topsy could become an angel as well as any of us, if she were a Christian?"

"Topsy! what a ridiculous idea! Nobody but you would ever think of it. I suppose she could, though."

"But, mamma, isn't God her father, as much as ours? Isn't Jesus her Saviour?"

"Well, that may be. I suppose God made everybody," said Marie. "Where is my smelling-bottle?"

"It's such a pity, – oh! *such* a pity!" said Eva, looking out on the distant lake, and speaking half to herself.

"What's a pity?" said Marie.

"Why, that any one, who could be a bright angel, and live with angels should go all down, down, down, and nobody help them! – oh, dear!"

"Well, we can't help it; it's no use worrying, Eva! I don't know what's to be done; we ought to be thankful for our own advantages."

"I hardly can be," said Eva, "I'm so sorry to think of poor folks that haven't any."

"That's odd enough," said Marie; – "I'm sure my religion makes me thankful for my advantages."

"Mamma," said Eva, "I want to have some of my hair cut off, – a good deal of it."

"What for?" said Marie.

"Mamma, I want to give some away to my friends, while I am able to give it to them myself. Won't you ask aunty to come and cut it for me?"

Marie raised her voice, and called Miss Ophelia, from the other room.

The child half rose from her pillow as she came in, and, shaking down her long golden-brown curls, said, rather playfully, "Come, aunty, shear the sheep!"

"What's that?" said St. Clare, who just then entered with some fruit he had been out to get for her.

"Papa, I just want aunty to cut off some of my hair, – there's too much of it, and it makes my head hot. Besides, I want to give some of it away."

Miss Ophelia came, with her scissors.

"Take care, – don't spoil the looks of it!" said her father, "cut underneath, where it won't show. Eva's curls are my pride."

"O, papa!" said Eva, sadly.

"Yes, and I want them kept handsome against the time I take you up to your uncle's plantation, to see Cousin Henrique," said St. Clare, in a gay tone.

"I shall never go there, papa, – I am going to a better country. O, do believe me! Don't you see, papa, that I get weaker, every day?" [. . .] "Papa, my strength fades away every day, and I know I must go. There are some things I want to say and do, – that I ought to do; and you are so unwilling to have me speak a word on this subject. But it must come; there's no putting it off. Do be willing I should speak now!"

"My child, I *am* willing!" said St. Clare, covering his eyes with one hand and holding up Eva's hand with the other.

"Then, I want to see all our people together. I have some things I *must* say to them," said Eva.

"*Well*," said St. Clare, in a tone of dry endurance.

Miss Ophelia despatched a messenger, and soon the whole of the servants were convened in the room.

Eva lay back on her pillows; her hair hanging loosely about her face, her crimson cheeks contrasting painfully with the intense whiteness of her complexion and the thin contour of her limbs and features, and her large, soul-like eyes fixed earnestly on every one.

The servants were struck with a sudden emotion. The spiritual face, the long locks of hair cut off and lying by her, her father's averted face and Marie's sobs, struck at once upon the feelings of a sensitive and impressible race; and, as they came in, they looked one on another, sighed, and shook their heads. There was a deep silence, like that of a funeral.

Eva raised herself, and looked long and earnestly round at every one. All looked sad and apprehensive. Many of the women hid their faces in their aprons.

"I sent for you all, my dear friends," said Eva, "because I love you. I love you all; and I have something to say to you, which I want you always to remember . . . I am going to leave you. In a few more weeks, you will see me no more –"

Here the child was interrupted by bursts of groans, sobs, and lamentations, which broke from all present, and in which her slender voice was lost entirely. She waited a moment, and then, speaking in a tone that checked the sobs of all, she said,

"If you love me, you must not interrupt me so. Listen to what I say. I want to speak to you about your souls . . . Many of you, I am afraid, are very careless. You are thinking only about this world. I want you to remember that there is a beautiful world, where Jesus is. I am going there, and you can go there. It is for you, as much as me. But, if you want to go there, you must not live idle, careless, thoughtless lives. You must be Christians. You must remember that each one of you can become angels, and be angels forever . . . If you want to be Christians, Jesus will help you. You must pray to him; you must read –"

The child checked herself, looked piteously at them, and said, sorrowfully,

"O, dear! you *can't* read, – poor souls!" and she hid her face in the pillow and sobbed, while many a smothered sob from those she was addressing, who were kneeling on the floor, aroused her.

"Never mind," she said, raising her face and smiling brightly through her tears, "I have prayed for you; and I know Jesus will help you, even if you can't read. Try all to do the best you can; pray every day; ask Him to help you, and get the Bible read to you whenever you can; and I think I shall see you all in heaven."

"Amen," was the murmured response from the lips of Tom and Mammy, and some of the elder ones, who belonged to the Methodist church. The younger and more thoughtless ones, for the time completely overcome, were sobbing, with their heads bowed upon their knees.

"I know," said Eva, "you all love me."

"Yes; oh, yes! indeed we do! Lord bless her!" was the involuntary answer of all.

"Yes, I know you do! There isn't one of you that hasn't always been very kind to me; and I want to give you something that when you look at, you shall always remember me. I'm going to give all of you a curl of my hair; and, when you look at it, think that I loved you and am gone to heaven, and that I want to see you all there."

It is impossible to describe the scene, as, with tears and sobs, they gathered round the little creature, and took from her hands what seemed to them a last mark of her love. They fell on their knees; they sobbed, and prayed, and kissed the hem of her garment; and the elder ones poured forth words of endearment, mingled in prayers and blessings, after the manner of their susceptible race.

As each one took their gift, Miss Ophelia, who was apprehensive for the effect of all this excitement on her little patient, signed to each one to pass out of the apartment. [. . .]

Eva soon lay like a wearied dove in her father's arms; and he, bending over her, soothed her by every tender word he could think of.

Marie rose and threw herself out of the apartment into her own, when she fell into violent hysterics.

"You didn't give me a curl, Eva," said her father, smiling sadly.

"They are all yours, papa," said she, smiling, – "yours and mamma's; and you must give dear aunty as many as she wants. I only gave them to our poor people myself, because you know, papa, they might be forgotten when I am gone, and because I hoped it might help them remember . . . You are a Christian, are you not, papa?" said Eva, doubtfully.

"Why do you ask me?"

"I don't know. You are so good, I don't see how you can help it."

"What is being a Christian, Eva?"

"Loving Christ most of all," said Eva.

"Do you, Eva?"

"Certainly I do."

"You never saw him," said St. Clare.

"That makes no difference," said Eva. "I believe him, and in a few days I shall *see* him;" and the young face grew fervent, radiant with joy.

St. Clare said no more. It was a feeling which he had seen before in his mother; but no chord within vibrated to it.

Eva, after this, declined rapidly; there was no more any doubt of the event; the fondest hope could not be blinded. Her beautiful room was avowedly a sick room; and Miss Ophelia day and night performed the duties of a nurse, – and never did her friends appreciate her value more than in that capacity. With so well-trained a hand and eye, such perfect adroitness and practice in every art which could promote neatness and comfort, and keep out of sight every disagreeable incident of sickness, – with such a perfect sense of time, such a clear, untroubled head, such exact accuracy in remembering every prescription and direction of the doctors, – she was everything to him. They who had shrugged their shoulders at her little peculiarities and setnesses,[1] so unlike the careless freedom of southern manners, acknowledged that now she was the exact person that was wanted.

Uncle Tom was much in Eva's room. The child suffered much from nervous restlessness, and it was a relief to her to be carried; and it was Tom's greatest delight to carry her little frail form in his arms, resting on a pillow, now up and down her room, now out into the verandah; and when the fresh sea-breezes blew from the lake, – and the child felt freshest in the morning, – he would sometimes walk with her under the orange-trees in the garden, or, sitting down in some of their old seats, sing to her their favorite old hymns.

Her father often did the same thing; but his frame was slighter, and when he was weary, Eva would say to him,

"O, papa, let Tom take me. Poor fellow! it pleases him; and you know it's all he can do now, and he wants to do something!"

"So do I, Eva!" said her father.

"Well, papa, you can do everything, and are everything to me. You read to me, – you sit up nights, – and Tom has only this one thing, and his singing; and I know, too, he does it easier than you can. He carries me so strong!"

The desire to do something was not confined to Tom. Every servant in the establishment showed the same feeling, and in their way did what they could. [. . .]

Eva had been unusually bright and cheerful, that afternoon, and had sat raised in her bed, and looked over all her little trinkets and precious things, and designated the friends to whom she would have them given; and her manner was more animated, and her voice more natural, than they had known it for weeks. Her father had been in, in the evening, and had said that Eva appeared more like her former self than ever she had done since her sickness; and when he kissed her for the night, he said to Miss Ophelia, – "Cousin, we may keep her with us, after all; she is certainly better;" and he had retired with a lighter heart in his bosom than he had had there for weeks.

But at midnight, – strange, mystic hour! – when the veil between the frail present and the eternal future grows thin, – then came the messenger!

There was a sound in that chamber, first of one who stepped quickly. It was Miss Ophelia, who had resolved to sit up all night with her little charge, and who, at the turn of the night, had discerned what experienced nurses significantly call "a change." The outer door was quickly opened, and Tom, who was watching outside, was on the alert, in a moment.

"Go for the doctor, Tom! lose not a moment," said Miss Ophelia, and, stepping across the room, she rapped at St. Clare's door.

"Cousin," she said, "I wish you would come."

Those words fell on his heart like clods upon a coffin. Why did they? He was up and in the room in an instant, and bending over Eva, who still slept.

---

1   Fixed behavior or mannerism.

What was it he saw that made his heart stand still? Why was no word spoken between the two? Thou canst say, who hast seen that same expression on the face dearest to thee; – that look indescribable, hopeless, unmistakable, that says to thee that thy beloved is no longer thine.

On the face of the child, however, there was no ghastly imprint, – only a high and almost sublime expression, – the overshadowing presence of spiritual natures, the dawning of immortal life in that childish soul.

They stood there so still, gazing upon her, that even the ticking of the watch seemed too loud. In a few moments, Tom returned, with the doctor. He entered, gave one look, and stood silent as the rest.

"When did this change take place?" said he, in a low whisper, to Miss Ophelia.

"About the turn of the night," was the reply.

Marie, roused by the entrance of the doctor, appeared, hurriedly, from the next room.

"Augustine! Cousin! – O! – what!" she hurriedly began.

"Hush!" said St. Clare, hoarsely; "*she is dying*!"

Mammy heard the words, and flew to awaken the servants. The house was soon roused, – lights were seen, footsteps heard, anxious faces thronged the verandah, and looked tearfully through the glass doors, but St. Clare heard and said nothing, – he saw only *that look* on the face of the little sleeper.

"O, if she would only wake, and speak once more!" he said; and, stooping over her, he spoke in her ear, – "Eva, darling!"

The large blue eyes unclosed, – a smile passed over her face; – she tried to raise her head, and to speak.

"Do you know me, Eva?"

"Dear papa," said the child, with a last effort, throwing her arms about his neck. In a moment they dropped again; and, as St. Clare raised his head, he saw a spasm of mortal agony pass over the face, – she struggled for breath, and threw up her little hands.

"Oh God, this is dreadful!" he said, turning away in agony, and wringing Tom's hand, scarce conscious what he was doing. "O, Tom, my boy, it is killing me!"

Tom had his master's hands between his own; and, with tears streaming down his dark cheeks, looked up for help where he had always been used to look.

"Pray that this may be cut short!" said St. Clare, – "this wrings my heart."

"O, bless the Lord! it's over, – it's over, dear Master!" said Tom; "look at her."

The child lay panting on her pillows, as one exhausted, – the large clear eyes rolled up and fixed. Ah, what said those eyes, that spoke so much of heaven? Earth was past, and earthly pain; but so solemn, so mysterious, was the triumphant brightness of that face, that it checked even the sobs of sorrow. They pressed around her, in breathless stillness.

"Eva," said St. Clare, gently.

She did not hear.

"O, Eva, tell us what you see! What is it?" said her father.

A bright, a glorious smile passed over her face, and she said, brokenly, – "O! love, – joy, – peace!" gave one sigh, and passed from death unto life!

"Farewell, beloved child! the bright, eternal doors have closed after thee; we shall see thy sweet face no more. O, woe for them who watched thy entrance into heaven, when they shall wake and find only the cold gray sky of daily life, and thou gone forever!"

Chapter 27: "This is the Last of Earth" – John Q. Adams[1]

Eva's deathbed lessons about love and Christ affect not only Topsy, St. Clare, and the attending slaves, but also Miss Ophelia. Up until this point, Miss Ophelia has been emotionally distant from, and slightly repulsed by, Topsy. Now the representative of northern womanhood has learned Eva's lesson about Christian love, and will love Topsy and raise her to be a good Christian.

[. . .] Topsy came forward and laid her offering at the feet of the corpse; then suddenly, with a wild and bitter cry, she threw herself on the floor alongside the bed, and wept, and moaned aloud.

Miss Ophelia hastened into the room, and tried to raise and silence her; but in vain.

"O, Miss Eva! oh, Miss Eva! I wish I's dead, too, – I do!"

There was a piercing wildness in the cry; the blood flushed into St. Clare's white, marble-like face, and the first tears he had shed since Eva died stood in his eyes.

"Get up, child," said Miss Ophelia, in a softened voice; "don't cry so. Miss Eva is gone to heaven; she is an angel."

"But I can't see her!" said Topsy. "I never shall see her!" and she sobbed again.

They all stood a moment in silence.

"She said she *loved* me," said Topsy, – "she did! O, dear! oh, dear! there an't *nobody* left now, – there an't!"

"That's true enough," said St. Clare; "but do," he said to Miss Ophelia, "see if you can't comfort the poor creature."

"I jist wish I hadn't never been born," said Topsy. "I didn't want to be born, no ways; and I don't see no use on't."

Miss Ophelia raised her gently, but firmly, and took her from the room; but, as she did so, some tears fell from her eyes.

---

1   The dying words of John Quincy Adams (1767–1848), the sixth President of the United States (1825–9) were "This is the last of earth! I am content."

"Topsy, you poor child," she said, as she led her into her room, "don't give up! *I* can love you, though I am not like that dear little child. I hope I've learnt something of the love of Christ from her. I can love you; I do, and I'll try to help you to grow up a good Christian girl."

Miss Ophelia's voice was more than her words, and more than that were the honest tears that fell down her face. From that hour, she acquired an influence over the mind of the destitute child that she never lost.

"O, my Eva, whose little hour on earth did so much of good," thought St. Clare, "what account have I to give for my long years?"

There were, for a while, soft whisperings and foot-falls in the chamber, as one after another stole in, to look at the dead; and then came the little coffin; and then there was a funeral, and carriages drove to the door, and strangers came and were seated; and there were white scarfs and ribbons, and crape bands, and mourners dressed in black crape; and there were words read from the Bible, and prayers offered; and St. Clare lived, and walked, and moved, as one who has shed every tear; – to the last he saw only one thing, that golden head in the coffin; but then he saw the cloth spread over it, the lid of the coffin closed; and he walked, when he was put beside the others, down to a little place at the bottom of the garden, and there, by the mossy seat where she and Tom had talked, and sung, and read so often, was the little grave. St. Clare stood beside it, – looked vacantly down; he saw them lower the little coffin; he heard, dimly, the solemn words, "I am the resurrection and the Life; he that believeth in me, though he were dead, yet shall he live;"[2] and, as the earth was cast in and filled up the little grave, he could not realize that it was his Eva that they were hiding from his sight.

Nor was it! – not Eva, but only the frail seed of that bright, immortal form with which she shall yet come forth, in the day of the Lord Jesus! [. . .]

Miss Ophelia asks her brother for legal ownership of Topsy so that she can bring Topsy north and free her. St. Clare signs Topsy over to Ophelia, who ironically becomes a slave owner. Ophelia urges St. Clare to make provisions for his other slaves in the event of his sudden death, because the slaves could then be sold to cruel slave masters. St. Clare agrees, but gets stabbed to death in a bar fight before he can address his slaves' needs. The slaves become the property of Marie, who commands that they all be sent to the slave warehouse to be sold at auction.

2   Christ says these words in John 11.25–6.

Chapter 30: The Slave Warehouse

Stowe strongly condemns the sale of human beings in this chapter by showing the reader the sale of Tom and two other slaves, Susan and her daughter Emmeline, in the degrading, dehumanizing conditions of a New Orleans slave warehouse. The cruel slave owner, Simon Legree, is introduced here.

A slave warehouse! Perhaps some of my readers conjure up horrible visions of such a place. They fancy some foul, obscure den [. . .] But no, innocent friend; in these days men have learned the art of sinning expertly and genteelly, so as not to shock the eyes and senses of respectable society. Human property is high in the market; and is, therefore, well fed, well cleaned, tended, and looked after, that it may come to sale sleek, and strong, and shining. A slave-warehouse in New Orleans is a house externally not much unlike many others, kept with neatness; and where every day you may see arranged, under a sort of shed along the outside, rows of men and women, who stand there as a sign of the property sold within.

Then you shall be courteously entreated to call and examine, and shall find an abundance of husbands, wives, brothers, sisters, fathers, mothers, and young children, to be "sold separately, or in lots to suit the convenience of the pur-chaser;" and that soul immortal, once bought with blood and anguish by the Son of God, when the earth shook, and the rocks rent, and the graves were opened, can be sold, leased, mortgaged, exchanged for groceries or dry goods, to suit the phases of trade, or the fancy of the purchaser. [. . .]

Tom had with him quite a sizable trunk full of clothing as had most others of them. They were ushered, for the night, into a long room, where many other men, of all ages, sizes and shades of complexion, were assembled, and from which roars of laughter and unthinking merriment were proceeding. [. . .]

The dealers in the human article make scrupulous and systematic efforts to promote noisy mirth among them, as a means of drowning reflection, and rendering them insensible to their condition. The whole object of the training to which the negro is put, from the time he is sold in the northern market till he arrives south, is systematically directed towards making him callous, unthinking, and brutal. The slave-dealer collects his gang in Virginia or Kentucky, and drives them to some convenient, healthy place, – often a watering place, – to be fattened. Here they are fed full daily; and, because some incline to pine, a fiddle is kept commonly going among them, and they are made to dance daily; and he who refuses to be merry – in whose soul thoughts of wife, or child, or home, are too strong for him to be gay – is marked as sullen and dangerous, and subjected to all the evils which the ill will of an utterly irresponsible and hardened man can inflict upon him. Briskness, alertness, and cheerfulness of appearance, especially before observers, are constantly enforced upon them, both by the hope of thereby getting a good master, and the fear of all that the driver may bring upon them, if they prove unsalable.

"What dat ar nigger doin here?" said Sambo, coming up to Tom, after Mr. Skeggs had left the room. Sambo was a full black, of great size, very lively, voluble, and full of trick and grimace.

"What you doin here?" said Sambo, coming up to Tom, and poking him facetiously in the side. "Meditatin', eh?"

"I am to be sold at the auction, to-morrow!" said Tom, quietly. [. . .]

[T]he reader may be curious to take a peep at the corresponding apartment allotted to the women. Stretched out in various attitudes over the floor, he may see numberless sleeping forms of every shade of complexion, from the purest ebony to white, and of all years, from childhood to old age, lying now asleep. Here is a fine bright girl, of ten years, whose mother was sold out yesterday, and who to-night cried herself to sleep when nobody was looking at her. Here, a worn old negress, whose thin arms and callous fingers tell of hard toil, waiting to be sold to-morrow, as a cast-off article, for what can be got for her; and some forty or fifty others with heads variously enveloped in blankets or articles of clothing, lie stretched around them. But, in a corner, sitting apart from the rest, are two females of a more interesting appearance than common. One of these is a respectably-dressed mulatto woman between forty and fifty, with soft eyes and a gentle and pleasing physiognomy. She has on her head a high-raised turban, made of a gay red Madras handkerchief, of the first quality, and her dress is neatly fitted, and of good material, showing that she has been provided for with a careful hand. By her side and nestling closely to her, is a young girl of fifteen, – her daughter. She is a quadroon,[1] as may be seen from her fairer complexion, though her likeness to her mother is quite discernible. She has the same soft, dark eye, with longer lashes, and her curling hair is of a luxuriant brown. She also is dressed with great neatness, and her white, delicate hands betray very little acquaintance with servile toil. These two are to be sold to-morrow, in the same lot with the St. Clare servants; and the gentleman to whom they belong, and to whom the money for their sale is to be transmitted, is a member of a Christian church in New York, who will receive the money, and go thereafter to the sacrament of his Lord and theirs, and think no more of it.

These two, whom we shall call Susan and Emmeline, had been the personal attendants of an amiable and pious lady of New Orleans, by whom they had been carefully and piously instructed and trained. They had been taught to read and write, diligently instructed in the truths of religion, and their lot had been as happy an one as in their condition it was possible to be. But the only son of their protectress had the management of her property; and, by carelessness and extravagance involved it to a large amount, and at last failed. [. . .]

Susan and Emmeline were [. . .] sent to the depot to await a general auction on the following morning; and as they glimmer faintly upon us in the moonlight which steals through the grated window, we may listen to their conversation. Both are weeping, but each quietly, that the other may not hear.

---

1   A person with one-fourth black ancestry.

"Mother, just lay your head on my lap, and see if you can't sleep a little," says the girl, trying to appear calm.

"I haven't any heart to sleep, Em; I can't; it's the last night we may be together!"

"O, mother, don't say so! perhaps we shall get sold together, – who knows?"

"If't was anybody's else case, I should say so, too, Em," said the woman; "but I'm so feard of losin' you that I don't see anything but the danger."

"Why, mother, the man said we were both likely, and would sell well."

Susan remembered the man's looks and words. With a deadly sickness at her heart, she remembered how he had looked at Emmeline's hands and lifted up her curly hair, and pronounced her a first-rate article. Susan had been trained as a Christian, brought up in the daily reading of the Bible, and had the same horror of her child's being sold to a life of shame that any other Christian mother might have; but she had no hope, – no protection.

"Mother, I think we might do first rate, if you could get a place as cook, and I as chamber-maid or seamstress, in some family. I dare say we shall. Let's both look as bright and lively as we can, and tell all we can do, and perhaps we shall," said Emmeline.

"I want you to brush your hair all back straight, to-morrow," said Susan.

"What for, mother? I don't look near so well, that way."

"Yes, but you'll sell better so."

"I don't see why!" said the child.

"Respectable families would be more apt to buy you, if they saw you looked plain and decent, as if you wasn't trying to look handsome. I know their ways better 'n you do," said Susan.

"Well, mother, then I will."

"And, Emmeline, if we shouldn't ever see each other again, after tomorrow, – if I'm sold way up on a plantation somewhere, and you somewhere else, – always remember how you've been brought up, and all Missis has told you; take your Bible with you, and your hymn-book; and if you're faithful to the Lord, he'll be faithful to you."

So speaks the poor soul, in sore discouragement; for she knows that to-morrow any man, however vile and brutal, however godless and merciless, if he only has money to pay for her, may become owner of her daughter, body and soul; and then, how is the child to be faithful? [. . .]

Tom had been standing wistfully examining the multitude of faces thronging around him, for one whom he would wish to call master. And if you should ever be under the necessity, sir, of selecting, out of two hundred men, one who was to become your absolute owner and disposer, you would, perhaps, realize, just as Tom did, how few there were that you would feel at all comfortable in being made over to. Tom saw abundance of men, – great, burly, gruff men; little, chirping, dried men; long-favored, lank, hard men; and every variety of stubbed-looking, commonplace men, who pick up their fellow-men as one picks up chips, putting them into the fire or a basket with equal unconcern, according to their convenience; but he saw no St. Clare.

A little before the sale commenced, a short, broad, muscular man, in a checked shirt considerably open at the bosom, and pantaloons much the worse for dirt and wear, elbowed his way through the crowd, like one who is going actively into a business; and, coming up to the group, began to examine them systematically. From the moment that Tom saw him approaching, he felt an immediate and revolting horror at him, that increased as he came near. He was evidently, though short, of gigantic strength. His round, bullet head, large, light-gray eyes, with their shaggy, sandy eye-brows, and stiff, wiry, sun-burned hair, were rather unprepossessing items, it is to be confessed; his large, coarse mouth was distended with tobacco, the juice of which, from time to time, he ejected from him with great decision and explosive force; his hands were immensely large, hairy, sunburned, freckled, and very dirty, and garnished with long nails, in a very foul condition. This man proceeded to a very free personal examination of the lot. He seized Tom by the jaw, and pulled open his mouth to inspect his teeth; made him strip up his sleeve, to show his muscle; turned him round, made him jump and spring, to show his paces.

"Where was you raised?" he added, briefly, to these investigations.

"In Kintuck, Mas'r," said Tom, looking about, as if for deliverance.

"What have you done?"

"Had care of Mas'r's farm," said Tom.

"Likely story!" said the other, shortly, as he passed on. He paused a moment [. . .] then spitting a discharge of tobacco-juice on his well-blacked boots, and giving a contemptuous umph, he walked on. Again he stopped before Susan and Emmeline. He put out his heavy, dirty hand, and drew the girl towards him; passed it over her neck and bust, felt her arms, looked at her teeth, and then pushed her back against her mother, whose patient face showed the suffering she had been going through at every motion of the hideous stranger.

The girl was frightened, and began to cry.

"Stop that, you minx!" said the salesman; "no whimpering here, – the sale is going to begin." And accordingly the sale begun.

Adolph was knocked off, at a good sum, to the young gentleman who had previously stated his intention of buying him; and the other servants of the St. Clare lot went to various bidders.

"Now, up with you, boy! d'ye hear?" said the auctioneer to Tom.

Tom stepped upon the block, gave a few anxious looks round; all seemed mingled in a common, indistinct noise, – the clatter of the salesman crying off his qualifications in French and English, the quick fire of French and English bids; and almost in a moment came the final thump of the hammer, and the clear ring on the last syllable of the word "*dollars*", as the auctioneer announced his price, and Tom was made over. – He had a master!

He was pushed from the block; – the short, bullet-headed man seizing him roughly by the shoulder, pushed him to one side, saying, in a harsh voice, "Stand there, *you*!"

Tom hardly realized anything; but still the bidding went on, – rattling, clattering, now French, now English. Down goes the hammer again, – Susan is sold! She goes down from the block, stops, looks wistfully back, – her daughter stretches her hands towards her. She looks with agony in the face of the man who has bought her, – a respectable middle-aged man, of benevolent countenance.

"O, Mas'r, please do buy my daughter!"

"I'd like to, but I'm afraid I can't afford it!" said the gentleman, looking, with painful interest, as the young girl mounted the block, and looked around her with a frightened and timid glance.

The blood flushes painfully in her otherwise colorless cheek, her eye has a feverish fire, and her mother groans to see that she looks more beautiful than she ever saw her before. The auctioneer sees his advantage, and expatiates volubly in mingled French and English, and bids rise in rapid succession.

"I'll do anything in reason," said the benevolent-looking gentleman, pressing in and joining with the bids. In a few moments they have run beyond his purse. He is silent; the auctioneer grows warmer; but bids gradually drop off. It lies now between an aristocratic old citizen and our bullet-headed acquaintance. The citizen bids for a few turns, contemptuously measuring his opponent; but the bullet-head has the advantage over him, both in obstinacy and concealed length of purse, and the controversy lasts but a moment; the hammer falls, – he has got the girl, body and soul, unless God help her!

Her master is Mr. Legree, who owns a cotton plantation on the Red river.[2] She is pushed along into the same lot with Tom and two other men, and goes off, weeping as she goes.

The benevolent gentleman is sorry; but, then, the thing happens every day! One sees girls and mothers crying, at these sales, *always!* it can't be helped, &c.; and he walks off, with his acquisition, in another direction. [. . .]

Stowe presents the hidden evils of such "kind" slave masters as St. Clare and the unambiguous evil of such cruel slave masters as Simon Legree. While working in the cotton fields, Tom notices Cassy having difficulty filling her sacks and assists her. Legree's slave and concubine, Cassy, in turn helps Tom. Angered that slaves help each other, Legree orders Tom to whip Cassy. Tom refuses and receives a horrible beating from Legree's overseers. Gillian Brown's essay addresses Cassy's plight (**pp. 48–51**).

Chapter 34: The Quadroon's Story

Cassy empathizes with Tom after his beating and confesses to him that her cruel experiences as a slave have forced her to give up on God. She tells Tom about her tragic life and her great sadness at having her children sold away from her.

---

2   A tributary of the Mississippi River.

[. . .] "It's no use, my poor fellow!" [Cassy] broke out, at last, "it's of no use this you've been trying to do. You were a brave fellow, – you had the right on your side; but it's all in vain, and out of the question, for you to struggle. You are in the devil's hands; – he is the strongest, and you must give up!"

Give up! and, had not human weakness and physical agony whispered that, before? Tom started; for the bitter woman, with her wild eyes and melancholy voice, seemed to him an embodiment of the temptation with which he had been wrestling.

"O Lord! O Lord!" he groaned, "how can I give up?"

"There's no use calling on the Lord, – he never hears," said the woman steadily; "there isn't any God, I believe; or, if there is, he's taken sides against us. All goes against us, heaven and earth. Everything is pushing us into hell. Why shouldn't we go?"

Tom closed his eyes, and shuddered at the dark, atheistic words.

"You see," said the woman, "*you* don't know anything about it; – I do. I've been on this place five years, body and soul, under this man's foot; and I hate him as I do the devil! Here you are, on a lone plantation ten miles from any other, in the swamps; not a white person here, who could testify, if you were burned alive, – if you were scalded, cut into inch-pieces, set up for the dogs to tear, or hung up and whipped to death. There's no law here, of God or man, that can do you, or any one of us, the least good; and, this man! there's no earthly thing that he's too good to do. I could make any one's hair rise, and their teeth chatter, if I should only tell what I've seen and been knowing to, here, – and it's no use resisting! Did I *want* to live with him? Wasn't I a woman delicately bred; and he – God in heaven! what was he, and is he? And yet, I've lived with him, these five years, and cursed every moment of my life, – night and day! And now, he's got a new one, – a young thing, only fifteen, and she brought up, she says, piously. Her good mistress taught her to read the Bible; and she's brought her Bible here – to hell with her!" – and the woman laughed a wild and doleful laugh, that rung, with a strange, supernatural sound, through the old ruined shed. [. . .]

"You see me now," she said, speaking to Tom very rapidly; "see what I am! Well, I was brought up in luxury, the first I remember is, playing about, when I was a child, in splendid parlors; – when I was kept dressed up like a doll, and company and visiters used to praise me. There was a garden opening from the saloon windows; and there I used to play hide-and-go-seek, under the orange-trees, with my brothers and sisters. I went to a convent, and there I learned music, French and embroidery, and what not; and when I was fourteen, I came out to my father's funeral. He died very suddenly, and when the property came to be settled, they found that there was scarcely enough to cover the debts; and when the creditors took an inventory of the property, I was set down in it. My mother was a slave woman, and my father had always meant to set me free; but he had not done it, and so I was set down in the list. I'd always known who I was, but never thought much about it. Nobody ever expects that a strong, healthy man is a going to die. My father was a well man only four hours before he died; – it was one of the first cholera cases in New Orleans. The day after the funeral, my father's wife took her children, and went up to her father's plantation. I thought they treated me strangely, but didn't know. There was a young lawyer who they left to settle the business and he came every day, and was about the house, and spoke very politely to me. He brought with him, one day, a young man, whom I thought the handsomest I had ever seen. I shall never forget that evening. I walked with him in the garden. I was lonesome and full of sorrow, and he was so kind and gentle to me; and he told me that he had seen me before I went to the convent, and that he had loved me a great while, and that he would be my friend and protector; – in short, though he didn't tell me, he had paid two thousand dollars for me, and I was his property, – I became his willingly, for I loved him. Loved!" said the woman, stopping. "O, how I *did* love that man! How I love him now, – and always shall, while I breathe! He was so beautiful, so high, so noble! He put me into a beautiful house, with servants, horses, and carriages, and furniture, and dresses. Everything that money could buy, he gave me; but I didn't set any value on all that, – I only cared for him. I loved him better than my God and my own soul; and, if I tried, I couldn't do any other way from what he wanted me to.

"I wanted only one thing – I did want him to *marry* me. I thought, if he loved me as he said he did, and if I was what he seemed to think I was, he would be willing to marry me and set me free. But he convinced me that it would be impossible; and he told me that, if we were only faithful to each other, it was marriage before God. If that is true, wasn't I that man's wife? Wasn't I faithful? For seven years, didn't I study every look and motion, and only live and breathe to please him? He had the yellow fever, and for twenty days and nights I watched with him. I alone, – and gave him all his medicine, and did everything for him; and then he called me his good angel, and said I'd saved his life. We had two beautiful children. The first was a boy, and we called him Henry. He was the image of his father, – he had such beautiful eyes, such a forehead, and his hair hung all in curls around it; and he had all his father's spirit, and his talent, too. Little Elise, he said, looked like me. He used to tell me that I was the most beautiful woman in Louisiana, he was so proud of me and the children. He used to love to have me dress them up, and take them and me about in an open carriage and hear the remarks that people would make on us; and he used to fill my ears constantly with the fine things that were said in praise of me and the children. O, those were happy days! I thought I was as happy as any one could be; but then there came evil times. He had a cousin come to New Orleans, who was his particular friend, – he thought all the world of him; – but, from the first time I saw him, I couldn't tell why, I dreaded him; for I felt sure he was going to bring misery on us. He got Henry to going out with him, and often he would not come home nights till two or three o'clock. I did not dare say a word; for Henry was so high-spirited, I was afraid to. He got him to the gaming-houses; and he was one of the sort that, when he once got a going there, there was no holding back. And then he introduced him to another lady, and I saw soon that his heart was gone from me. He never told me, but I saw it, – I knew it day after day, – I felt my heart breaking, but I could not say a word! At this, the wretch offered to buy me and the children of Henry, to clear off his gambling debts, which stood in the way of his marrying as he wished; – and *he sold us*. He told me, one day, that he had business in the country, and should be gone two or three weeks. He spoke kinder than usual, and said he should come back; but it didn't deceive me. I knew that the time had come; I was just like one turned into stone; I couldn't speak, nor shed a tear. He kissed me and kissed the children, a good many times, and went out. I saw him get on his horse, and I watched him till he was quite out of sight; and then I fell down, and fainted.

"Then *he* came, the cursed wretch! he came to take possession. He told me that he had bought me and my children; and showed me the papers. I cursed him before God, and told him I'd die sooner than live with him.

"'Just as you please,' said he; 'but, if you don't behave reasonably, I'll sell both the children, where you shall never see them again.' He told me that he always had meant to have me, from the first time he saw me and that he had drawn Henry on, and got him in debt, on purpose to make him willing to sell me. That he got him in love with another woman; and that I might know, after all that, that he should not give up for a few airs and tears, and things of that sort.

"I gave up, for my hands were tied. He had my children, – whenever I resisted his will anywhere, he would talk about selling them and he made me as submissive as he desired. [. . .] I tried to keep them apart, for I held on to those children like death; but it did no good. *He sold both those children.* [. . .] One day, I was out walking, and passed by the calaboose; I saw a crowd about the gate, and heard a child's voice, – and suddenly my Henry broke away from two or three men who were holding him, and ran, screaming, and caught my dress. They came up to him, swearing dreadfully; and one man, whose face I shall never forget, told him that he wouldn't get away so; that he was going with him into the calaboose, and he'd get a lesson there he'd never forget. I tried to beg and plead, – they only laughed; the poor boy screamed and looked into my face, and held on to me, until, in tearing him off, they tore the skirt of my dress half away; and they carried him in, screaming 'Mother! mother! mother!' [. . .]

"It seemed to me something in my head snapped, at that moment. I felt dizzy and furious. I remember seeing a great sharp bowie-knife on the table; I remember something about catching it, and flying upon him; and then all grew dark, and I didn't know any more – not for days and days. [. . .]

"At length, one day, came a gentleman named Stuart. He seemed to have some feeling for me; he saw that something dreadful was on my heart, and he came to see me alone, a great many times, and finally persuaded me to tell him. He bought me, at last, and promised to do all he could to find and buy back my children. He went to the hotel where my Henry was; they told him he had been sold to a planter up on Pearl river;[1] that was the last that I ever heard. Then he found where my daughter was; an old woman was keeping her. He offered an immense sum for

---

1   A river in the center of the state of Mississippi.

her, but they would not sell her. Butler found out that it was for me he wanted her; and he sent me word that I should never have her. Captain Stuart was very kind to me; he had a splendid plantation, and took me to it. In the course of a year, I had a son born. O, that child! – how I loved it! How just like my poor Henry the little thing looked! But I had made up my mind, – yes, I had. I would never again let a child live to grow up! I took the little fellow in my arms, when he was two weeks old, and kissed him, and cried over him; and then I gave him laudanum, and held him close to my bosom, while he slept to death. How I mourned and cried over it! and who ever dreamed that it was anything but a mistake, that had made me give it the laudanum? but it's one of the few things that I'm glad of, now. I am not sorry, to this day; he, at least, is out of pain. What better than death could I give him, poor child! After a while, the cholera came, and Captain Stuart died; everybody died that wanted to live, – and I, – I, though I went down to death's door, – I *lived!* Then I was sold and passed from hand to hand, till I grew faded and wrinkled, and I had a fever; and then this wretch bought me, and brought me here, – and here I am!"

> Legree's jeers and beatings weaken Tom's faith, but singing religious hymns fortifies his beliefs. Cassy reveals to Tom her desire to kill Legree, but Tom persuades her to run away instead. Playing upon Legree's fear of ghosts, Cassy and Emmeline make Legree think the garret of his house is haunted. The two slave women escape to the swamp; as the search party looks for them, they sneak back into the "haunted" garret, confident that Legree will not venture to that part of the house.

Chapter 40: The Martyr

> Legree suspects that Tom knows information regarding the slaves' escape, but Tom states he would rather be beaten to death than reveal the women's whereabouts. Legree cruelly strikes Tom down to the ground. As the slaves Quimbo and Sambo wash Tom's wounds, they ask him about Jesus. Once again in the novel, a believer dies and, Christ-like, helps save the souls of others.

[. . .] The escape of Cassy and Emmeline irritated the before surly temper of Legree to the last degree; and his fury, as was to be expected, fell upon the defenceless head of Tom. [. . .] [H]e knew all the plan of the fugitives' escape, and the place of their present concealment; – he knew the deadly character of the man he had to deal with, and his despotic power. But he felt strong in God to meet death, rather than betray the helpless.

He sat his basket down by the row, and, looking up, said, "Into thy hands I commend my spirit! Thou hast redeemed me, oh Lord God of truth!"[1] [. . .]

"Well, Tom!" said Legree, walking up, and seizing him grimly by the collar of his coat, and speaking through his teeth, in a paroxysm of determined rage, "do you know I've made up my mind to KILL you?"

"It's very likely, Mas'r," said Tom, calmly.

"I *have*," said Legree, with grim, terrible calmness, "*done – just – that – thing*, Tom, unless you'll tell me what you know about these yer gals!"

Tom stood silent.

"D' ye hear?" said Legree, stamping, with a roar like that of an incensed lion. "Speak!"

"*I han't got nothing to tell, Mas'r*," said Tom, with a slow, firm deliberate utterance.

"Do you dare to tell me, ye old black Christian, ye don't *know*?" said Legree. Tom was silent.

"Speak!" thundered Legree, striking him furiously. "Do you know anything?"

"I know, Mas'r; but I can't tell anything. *I can die!*"

Legree drew in a long breath; and, suppressing his rage, took Tom by the arm, and, approaching his face almost to his, said, in a terrible voice, "Hark'e, Tom! – ye think, 'cause I've let you off before, I don't mean what I say; but, this time, I've *made up my mind*, and counted the cost. You've always stood it out agin' me: now, I'll *conquer ye, or kill ye!* – one or t'other. I'll count every drop of blood there is in you, and take 'em, one by one, till ye give up!"

Tom looked up to his master, and answered, "Mas'r, if you was sick or in trouble, or dying, and I could save ye, I'd *give* ye my heart's blood and, if taking every drop of blood in this poor old body would save your precious soul, I'd give 'em freely, as the Lord gave his for me. O, Mas'r! don't bring this great sin on your soul! It will hurt you more than 't will me! Do the worst you can, my troubles'll be over soon; but, if ye don't repent, yours won't *never* end!"

Like a strange snatch of heavenly music, heard in the lull of a tempest, this burst of feeling made a moment's blank pause. Legree stood aghast, and looked at Tom; and there was such a silence, that the tick of the old clock could be heard, measuring, with silent touch, the last moments of mercy and probation to that hardened heart.

It was but a moment. There was one hesitating pause, – one irresolute, relenting thrill, – and the spirit of evil came back, with seven-fold vehemence; and Legree, foaming with rage, smote his victim to the ground.

Scenes of blood and cruelty are shocking to our ear and heart. What man has nerve to do, man has not nerve to hear. What brother-man and brother-Christian must suffer, cannot be told us, even in our secret chamber, it so harrows up the soul! And yet, oh my country! these things are done under the shadow of thy laws! O, Christ! thy church sees them, almost in silence!

---

1   In Luke 23.46, Christ speaks his last words on the cross: "Father, into thy hands I commend my spirit."

But, of old, there was One whose suffering changed an instrument of torture, degradation and shame, into a symbol of glory, honor, and immortal life; and, where His spirit is, neither degrading stripes, nor blood, nor insults, can make the Christian's last struggle less than glorious.

Was he alone, that long night, whose brave, loving spirit was bearing up, in that old shed, against buffeting and brutal stripes?

Nay! There stood by him ONE, – seen by him alone, – "like unto the Son of God."

The tempter stood by him, too, – blinded by furious, despotic will, – every moment pressing him to shun that agony by the betrayal of the innocent. But the brave, true heart was firm on the Eternal Rock. Like his Master, he knew that, if he saved others, himself he could not save; nor could utmost extremity wring from him words, save of prayer and holy trust.

"He's most gone, Mas'r," said Sambo, touched, in spite of himself, by the patience of his victim.

"Pay away, till he gives up! Give it to him! – give it to him!" shouted Legree. "I'll take every drop of blood he has, unless he confesses!"

Tom opened his eyes, and looked upon his master. "Ye poor miserable critter!" he said, "there an't no more ye can do! I forgive ye, with all my soul!" and he fainted entirely away.

"I b'lieve, my soul, he's done for, finally," said Legree, stepping forward, to look at him. "Yes, he is! Well, his mouth's shut up, at last, – that's one comfort!"

Yes, Legree; but who shall shut up that voice in thy soul? that soul, past repentance, past prayer, past hope, in whom the fire that never shall be quenched is already burning!

Yet Tom was not quite gone. His wondrous words and pious prayers had struck upon the hearts of the imbruted blacks, who had been the instruments of cruelty upon him; and, the instant Legree withdrew, they took him down, and, in their ignorance, sought to call him back to life, – as if *that* were any favor to him.

"Sartin, we's been doin' a dreffle wicked thing!" said Sambo; "hopes Mas'r'll have to 'count for it, and not we."

They washed his wounds, – they provided a rude bed, of some refuse cotton, for him to lie down on; and one of them, stealing up to the house, begged a drink of brandy of Legree, pretending that he was tired, and wanted it for himself. He brought it back, and poured it down Tom's throat.

"O, Tom!" said Quimbo, "we's been awful wicked to ye!"

"I forgive ye, with all my heart!" said Tom, faintly.

"O, Tom! do tell us who is *Jesus*, anyhow?" said Sambo; – "Jesus, that's been a standin' by you so, all this night! – Who is he?"

The word roused the failing, fainting spirit. He poured forth a few energetic sentences of that wondrous One, – his life, his death, his everlasting presence, and power to save.

They wept, – both the two savage men.

"Why didn't I never hear this before?" said Sambo; "but I do believe! – I can't help it! Lord Jesus, have mercy on us!"

"Poor critters!" said Tom, "I'd be willing to bar' all I have, if it'll only bring ye to Christ! O, Lord! give me these two more souls, I pray!"

That prayer was answered!

Chapter 41: The Young Master

Young George Shelby, Jr., the son of Tom's former master, arrives on Legree's plantation in search of Uncle Tom in order to buy him and restore him to his cabin on the Kentucky plantation where his wife, Chloe, awaits him. Tom's death inspires George to resolve to do what he can to abolish slavery.

Two days after, a young man drove a light wagon up through the avenue of china-trees, and, throwing the reins hastily on the horses' neck, sprang out and inquired for the owner of the place. [. . .] He was soon introduced into the house, where he found Legree in the sitting-room.

Legree received the stranger with a kind of surly hospitality.

"I understand," said the young man, "that you bought, in New Orleans, a boy, named Tom. He used to be on my father's place, and I came to see if I couldn't buy him back."

Legree's brow grew dark, and he broke out, passionately: "Yes, I did buy such a fellow, – and a h—l of a bargain I had of it, too! The most rebellious, saucy, impudent dog! Set up my niggers to run away; got off two gals, worth eight hundred or a thousand dollars apiece. He owned to that, and, when I bid him tell me where they was, he up and said he knew, but he wouldn't tell; and stood to it, though I gave him the cussedest flogging I ever gave nigger yet. I b'lieve he's trying to die; but I don't know as he'll make it out."

"Where is he?" said George, impetuously. "Let me see him." The cheeks of the young man were crimson, and his eyes flashed fire; but he prudently said nothing, as yet.

"He's in dat ar shed," said a little fellow, who stood holding George's horse.

Legree kicked the boy, and swore at him; but George, without saying another word, turned and strode to the spot.

Tom had been lying two days since the fatal night; not suffering, for every nerve of suffering was blunted and destroyed. He lay, for the most part, in a quiet stupor; for the laws of a powerful and well-knit frame would not at once release the imprisoned spirit. By stealth, there had been there, in the darkness of the night, poor desolated creatures, who stole from their scanty hours' rest, that they might repay to him some of those ministrations of love in which he had always been so abundant. Truly, those poor disciples had little to give, – only the cup of cold water; but it was given with full hearts.

Tears had fallen on that honest, insensible face, – tears of late repentance in the poor, ignorant heathen, whom his dying love and patience had awakened to repentance, and bitter prayers, breathed over him to a late-found Saviour, of whom they scarce knew more than the name, but whom the yearning ignorant heart of man never implores in vain.

Cassy, who had glided out of her place of concealment, and, by overhearing, learned the sacrifice that had been made for her and Emmeline, had been there, the night before, defying the danger of detection; and, moved by the few last words which the affectionate soul had yet strength to breathe, the long winter of despair, the ice of years, had given way, and the dark, despairing woman had wept and prayed.

When George entered the shed, he felt his head giddy and his heart sick.

"Is it possible, – is it possible?" said he, kneeling down by him. "Uncle Tom, my poor, poor old friend!" [. . .]

Tears which did honor to his manly heart fell from the young man's eyes, as he bent over his poor friend.

"O, dear Uncle Tom! do wake, – do speak once more! Look up! Here's Mas'r George, – your own little Mas'r George. Don't you know me?"

"Mas'r George!" said Tom, opening his eyes, and speaking in a feeble voice; "Mas'r George!" He looked bewildered.

Slowly the idea seemed to fill his soul; and the vacant eye became fixed and brightened, the whole face lighted up, the hard hands clasped, and tears ran down the cheeks.

"Bless the Lord! it is, – it is, – it's all I wanted! They haven't forgot me. It warms my soul; it does my old heart good! Now I shall die content! Bless the Lord, oh my soul!"

"You shan't die! you *mustn't* die, nor think of it! I've come to buy you, and take you home," said George, with impetuous vehemence.

"O, Mas'r George, ye're too late. The Lord's bought me, and is going to take me home, – and I long to go. Heaven is better than Kintuck."

"O, don't die! It'll kill me! – it'll break my heart to think what you've suffered, – and lying in this old shed, here! Poor, poor fellow!"

"Don't call me poor fellow!" said Tom, solemnly. "I *have* been poor fellow; but that's all past and gone, now. I'm right in the door, going into glory! O, Mas'r George! *Heaven has come!* I've got the victory! – the Lord Jesus has given it to me! Glory be to His name!"

George was awe-struck at the force, the vehemence, the power, with which these broken sentences were uttered. He sat gazing in silence.

Tom grasped his hand, and continued, – "Ye mustn't, now, tell Chloe, poor soul! how ye found me; – 't would be so dreful to her. Only tell her ye found me going into glory; and that I couldn't stay for no one. And tell her the Lord's stood by me everywhere and al'ays, and made everything light and easy. And oh, the poor chil'en, and the baby! – my old heart's been most broke for 'em, time and agin! Tell 'em all to follow me – follow me! Give my love to Mas'r, and dear good Missis, and everybody in the place! Ye don't know! 'Pears like I loves 'em all! I loves every creatur' everywhar! – it's nothing *but* love! O, Mas'r George! what a thing 't is to be a Christian!"

At this moment, Legree sauntered up to the door of the shed, looked in, with a dogged air of affected carelessness, and turned away.

"The old satan!" said George, in his indignation. "It's a comfort to think the devil will pay *him* for this, some of these days!"

"O, don't! – oh, ye mustn't!" said Tom, grasping his hand; "he's a poor mis'able critter! it's awful to think on't! O, if he only could repent, the Lord would forgive him now; but I'm 'feared he never will!"

"I hope he won't!" said George; "I never want to see *him* in heaven!"

"Hush, Mas'r George! – it worries me! Don't feel so! He an't done me no real harm, – only opened the gate of the kingdom for me; that's all!"

At this moment, the sudden flush of strength which the joy of meeting his young master had infused into the dying man gave way. A sudden sinking fell upon him; he closed his eyes; and that mysterious and sublime change passed over his face, that told the approach of other worlds.

He began to draw his breath with long, deep inspirations; and his broad chest rose and fell, heavily. The expression of his face was that of a conqueror. [. . .]

George sat fixed with solemn awe. It seemed to him that the place was holy; and, as he closed the lifeless eyes, and rose up from the dead, only one thought possessed him, – that expressed by his simple old friend, – "What a thing it is to be a Christian!"

He turned: Legree was standing, sullenly, behind him.

Something in that dying scene had checked the natural fierceness of youthful passion. The presence of the man was simply loathsome to George; and he felt only an impulse to get away from him, with as few words as possible.

Fixing his keen dark eyes on Legree, he simply said, pointing to the dead, "You have got all you ever can of him. What shall I pay you for the body? I will take it away, and bury it decently."

"I don't sell dead niggers," said Legree, doggedly. "You are welcome to bury him where and when you like."

"Boys," said George, in an authoritative tone, to two or three negroes, who were looking at the body, "help me lift him up, and carry him to my wagon; and get me a spade."

One of them ran for a spade; the other two assisted George to carry the body to the wagon.

George neither spoke to nor looked at Legree, who did not countermand his orders, but stood, whistling, with an air of forced unconcern. He sulkily followed them to where the wagon stood at the door.

George spread his cloak in the wagon, and had the body carefully disposed of in it, – moving the seat, so as to give it room. Then he turned, fixed his eyes on Legree, and said, with forced composure,

"I have not, as yet, said to you what I think of this most atrocious affair; – this is not the time and place. But, sir, this innocent blood shall have justice. I will proclaim this murder. I will go to the very first magistrate, and expose you."

"Do!" said Legree, snapping his fingers, scornfully. "I'd like to see you doing it. Where you going to get witnesses? – how you going to prove it? – Come, now!"

George saw, at once, the force of this defiance. There was not a white person on the place; and, in all southern courts, the testimony of colored blood is nothing. He felt, at that moment, as if he could have rent the heavens with his heart's indignant cry for justice; but in vain.

"After all, what a fuss, for a dead nigger!" said Legree.

The word was as a spark to a powder magazine. Prudence was never a cardinal virtue of the Kentucky boy. George turned, and, with one indignant blow, knocked Legree flat upon his face; and, as he stood over him, blazing with wrath and defiance, he would have formed no bad personification of his great namesake triumphing over the dragon.

Some men, however, are decidedly bettered by being knocked down. If a man lays them fairly flat in the dust, they seem immediately to conceive a respect for him; and Legree was one of this sort. As he rose, therefore, and brushed the dust from his clothes, he eyed the slowly retreating wagon with some evident consideration; nor did he open his mouth till it was out of sight.

Beyond the boundaries of the plantation, George had noticed a dry, sandy knoll, shaded by a few trees: there they made the grave.

"Shall we take off the cloak, Mas'r?" said the negroes, when the grave was ready.

"No, no, – bury it with him! It's all I can give you, now, poor Tom, and you shall have it."

They laid him in; and the men shovelled away, silently. They banked it up, and laid green turf over it.

"You may go, boys," said George, slipping a quarter[1] into the hand of each. They lingered about, however.

"If young Mas'r would please buy us – " said one.

"We'd serve him so faithful!" said the other.

"Hard times here, Mas'r!" said the first. "Do, Mas'r, buy us, please!"

"I can't! – I can't!" said George, with difficulty, motioning them off; "it's impossible!"

The poor fellows looked dejected, and walked off in silence.

"Witness, eternal God!" said George, kneeling on the grave of his poor friend; "oh, witness, that, from this hour, I will do *what one man can* to drive out this curse of slavery from my land!"

There is no monument to mark the last resting-place of our friend. He needs none! His Lord knows where he lies, and will raise him up, immortal, to appear with him when he shall appear in his glory.

Pity him not! Such a life and death is not for pity! Not in the riches of omnipotence is the chief glory of God; but in self-denying, suffering love! And blessed are the men whom he calls to fellowship with him, bearing their cross after him with patience. Of such it is written, "Blessed are they that mourn, for they shall be comforted."[2]

---

1   A generous sum of money in 1852.
2   Derived from Christ's Sermon on the Mount (Matthew 5.3–5).

In a series of unbelievable coincidences, Cassy and Emmeline, as they escape from Legree's plantation, happen to board the same ship as George Shelby, Mr. Shelby's son, who is on his way back to Kentucky. They meet Madame de Thoux, who realizes she may be George Harris's sister. As well, Cassy believes that Eliza Harris may be her long-lost daughter, Elise. While some present-day readers may sneer at what seems like an overly contrived plot, readers in the 1850s understood Stowe's heartfelt message that slavery tears apart families.

Chapter 43: Results

After a happy family reunion, they all move to France, using the money of George Harris's sister, Madame de Thoux, so that George can pursue an education. In a letter he writes to a friend, George explains that he longs for an African national identity and will therefore relocate his family to Liberia. Stowe received some harsh criticism for this seeming endorsement of the colonizationist movement; that is, Stowe portrays George as better off in Africa. Stowe fails to imagine George, or any freed black, as remaining in the United States as a useful citizen. Even Topsy becomes a missionary in Africa.

The rest of our story is soon told. George Shelby, interested, as any other young man might be, by the romance of the incident, no less than by feelings of humanity, was at the pains to send to Cassy the bill of sale of Eliza; whose date and name all corresponded with her own knowledge of facts, and left no doubt upon her mind as to the identity of her child. [. . .]

At this moment, there is a rap at the door; and Eliza goes and opens it. The delighted – "Why! – this you?" calls up her husband; and the good pastor of Amherstberg is welcomed. There are two more women with him, and Eliza asks them to sit down.

Now, if the truth must be told, the honest pastor had arranged a little programme, according to which this affair was to develop itself; and, on the way up, all had very cautiously and prudently exhorted each other not to let things out, except according to previous arrangement.

What was the good man's consternation, therefore, just as he had motioned to the ladies to be seated, and was taking out his pocket-handkerchief to wipe his mouth, so as to proceed to his introductory speech in good order, when Madame de Thoux upset the whole plan, by throwing her arms around George's neck, and letting all out at once, by saying, "O, George! don't you know me? I'm your sister Emily."

Cassy had seated herself more composedly, and would have carried on her part very well, had not little Eliza suddenly appeared before her in exact shape and form, every outline and curl, just as her daughter was when she saw her last. The little thing peered up in her face; and Cassy caught her up in her arms, pressed her to her bosom, saying, what at the moment she really believed, "Darling, I'm your mother!"

In fact, it was a troublesome matter to do up exactly in proper order; but the good pastor, at last, succeeded in getting everybody quiet, and delivering the speech with which he had intended to open the exercises; and in which, at last, he succeeded so well, that his whole audience were sobbing about him in a manner that ought to satisfy any orator, ancient or modern.

They knelt together, and the good man prayed, – for there are some feelings so agitated and tumultuous, that they can find rest only by being poured into the bosom of Almighty love, – and then, rising up, the new-found family embraced each other, with a holy trust in Him, who from such peril and dangers, and by such unknown ways, had brought them together. [. . .]

And, indeed, in two or three days, such a change has passed over Cassy, that our readers would scarcely know her. The despairing, haggard expression of her face had given way to one of gentle trust. She seemed to sink, at once, into the bosom of the family, and take the little ones into her heart, as something for which it long had waited. Indeed, her love seemed to flow more naturally to the little Eliza than to her own daughter; for she was the exact image and body of the child whom she had lost. The little one was a flowery bond between mother and daughter, through whom grew up acquaintanceship and affection. Eliza's steady, consistent piety, regulated by the constant reading of the sacred word, made her a proper guide for the shattered and wearied mind of her mother. Cassy yielded at once, and with her whole soul, to every good influence, and became a devout and tender Christian.

After a day or two, Madame de Thoux told her brother more particularly of her affairs. The death of her husband had left her an ample fortune, which she generously offered to share with the family. When she asked George what way she could best apply it for him, he answered, "Give me an education, Emily; that has always been my heart's desire. Then, I can do all the rest."

On mature deliberation, it was decided that the whole family should go, for some years, to France; whither they sailed, carrying Emmeline with them.

The good looks of the latter won the affection of the first mate of the vessel; and, shortly after entering the port, she became his wife.

George remained four years at a French university, and, applying himself with an unintermitted zeal, obtained a very thorough education.

Political troubles in France, at last, led the family again to seek an asylum in [Canada].

George's feelings and views, as an educated man, may be best expressed in a letter to one of his friends.

"I feel somewhat at a loss, as to my future course. True, as you have said to me, I might mingle in the circles of the whites, in this country, my shade of color is so slight, and that of my wife and family scarce perceptible. Well, perhaps, on sufferance, I might. But, to tell you the truth, I have no wish to.

"My sympathies are not for my father's race, but for my mother's. To him I was no more than a fine dog or horse: to my poor heart-broken mother I was a *child*; and, though I never saw her, after the cruel sale that separated us, till she died, yet I *know* she always loved me dearly. I know it by my own heart. When I think of all she suffered, of my own early sufferings, of the distresses and struggles of my heroic wife, of my sister, sold in the New Orleans slave-market, – though I hope to have no unchristian sentiments, yet I may be excused for saying, I have no wish to pass for an American, or to identify myself with them.

"It is with the oppressed, enslaved African race that I cast in my lot; and, if I wished anything, I would wish myself two shades darker, rather than one lighter.

"The desire and yearning of my soul is for an African *nationality*. I want a people that shall have a tangible, separate existence of its own; and where am I to look for it? Not in Hayti; for in Hayti they had nothing to start with. A stream cannot rise above its fountain. The race that formed the character of the Haytiens was a worn-out, effeminate one; and, of course, the subject race will be centuries in rising to anything.

"Where, then, shall I look? On the shores of Africa I see a republic,[1] – a republic formed of picked men, who, by energy and self-educating force, have, in many cases, individually, raised themselves above a condition of slavery. [. . .]"

George, with his wife, children, sister and mother, embarked for Africa, some few weeks after. If we are not mistaken, the world will yet hear from him there.

Of our other characters we have nothing very particular to write, except a word relating to Miss Ophelia and Topsy, and a farewell chapter, which we shall dedicate to George Shelby.

Miss Ophelia took Topsy home to Vermont with her, much to the surprise of that grave deliberative body whom a New Englander recognizes under the term "*Our folks.*" "Our folks," at first, thought it an odd and unnecessary addition to their well-trained domestic establishment; but, so thoroughly efficient was Miss Ophelia in her conscientious endeavor to do her duty by her elève,[2] that the child rapidly grew in grace and in favor with the family and neighborhood. At the age of womanhood, she was, by her own request, baptized, and became a member of the Christian church in the place, and showed so much intelligence, activity and zeal, and desire to do good in the world, that she was at last recommended, and approved, as a missionary to one of the stations in Africa; and we have heard that the same activity and ingenuity which, when a child, made her so multiform and restless in her developments, is now employed, in a safer and wholesomer manner, in teaching the children of her own country. [. . .]

---

1   The American Colonization Society established, in 1822, a colony on the west coast of Africa that in 1847 became the independent nation of Liberia. Stowe and others have been criticized for advocating that freed blacks emigrate to Africa rather than remain in the United States with the full rights and privileges of a citizen.

2   Pupil, student (French).

Chapter 45: Concluding Remarks

In the novel's final chapter, Stowe uses all of her rhetorical power to deliver what amounts to a sermon. She speaks directly to readers, exhorting them to realize that slavery contradicts Christian teaching. Stowe specifically addresses mothers and appeals to maternal sentiment to drive home her antislavery message. Note the novel's final Christian vision that seemingly offers housewives and mothers a way to combat slavery: they can "feel right" in their hearts and pray for social and religious change.

The writer has often been inquired of, by correspondents from different parts of the country, whether this narrative is a true one; and to these inquiries she will give one general answer.[1]

The separate incidents that compose the narrative are, to a very great extent, authentic, occurring, many of them, either under her own observation, or that of her personal friends. She or her friends have observed characters the counterpart of almost all that are here introduced; and many of the sayings are word for word as heard herself, or reported to her.

The personal appearance of Eliza, the character ascribed to her, are sketches drawn from life. The incorruptible fidelity, piety and honesty, of Uncle Tom, had more than one development, to her personal knowledge. Some of the most deeply tragic and romantic, some of the most terrible incidents, have also their parallel in reality. The incident of the mother's crossing the Ohio river on the ice is a well-known fact.[2] [. . .]

The author hopes she has done justice to that nobility, generosity, and humanity, which in many cases characterize individuals at the South. Such instances save us from utter despair of our kind. But, she asks any person, who knows the world, are such characters *common*, anywhere?

For many years of her life, the author avoided all reading upon or allusion to the subject of slavery, considering it as too painful to be inquired into, and one which advancing light and civilization would certainly live down. But, since the legislative act of 1850, when she heard, with perfect surprise and consternation, Christian and humane people actually recommending the remanding escaped fugitives into slavery, as a duty binding on good citizens, – when she heard, on all hands, from kind, compassionate and estimable people, in the free states of the North, deliberations and discussions as to what Christian duty could be on this head, – she could only think, These men and Christians cannot know what slavery is; if they did, such a question could never be open for discussion. And from this arose a desire to exhibit it in a *living dramatic reality*. She has endeavored to show

---

1   As the novel was appearing in weekly installments from June 1851 to April 1852 in the antislavery newspaper *The National Era*, readers wrote to inquire about the truth of the events in the story. Stowe here addresses readers' questions.

2   Stowe documents a similar account in her *A Key to Uncle Tom's Cabin*.

it fairly, in its best and its worst phases. In its *best* aspect, she has, perhaps, been successful; but, oh! who shall say what yet remains untold in that valley and shadow of death, that lies on the other side?

To you, generous, noble-minded men and women, of the South, – you, whose virtue, and magnanimity, and purity of character, are the greater for the severer trial it has encountered, – to you is her appeal. Have you not, in your own secret souls, in your own private conversings, felt that there are woes and evils, in this accursed system, far beyond what are here shadowed, or can be shadowed? Can it be otherwise? [. . .]

The writer has given only a faint shadow, a dim picture, of the anguish and despair that are, at this very moment, riving thousands of hearts, shattering thousands of families, and driving a helpless and sensitive race to frenzy and despair. There are those living who know the mothers whom this accursed traffic has driven to the murder of their children; and themselves seeking in death a shelter from woes more dreaded than death. Nothing of tragedy can be written, can be spoken, can be conceived, that equals the frightful reality of scenes daily and hourly acting on our shores, beneath the shadow of American law, and the shadow of the cross of Christ.

And now, men and women of America, is this a thing to be trifled with, apologized for, and passed over in silence? Farmers of Massachusetts, of New Hampshire, of Vermont, of Connecticut, who read this book by the blaze of your winter-evening fire, – strong-hearted, generous sailors and ship-owners of Maine, – is this a thing for you to countenance and encourage? Brave and generous men of New York, farmers of rich and joyous Ohio, and ye of the wide prairie states, – answer, is this a thing for you to protect and countenance? And you, mothers of America, – you, who have learned, by the cradles of your own children, to love and feel for all mankind, – by the sacred love you bear your child; by your joy in his beautiful, spotless infancy; by the motherly pity and tenderness with which you guide his growing years; by the anxieties of his education; by the prayers you breathe for his soul's eternal good; – I beseech you, pity the mother who has all your affections, and not one legal right to protect, guide, or educate, the child of her bosom! By the sick hour of your child; by those dying eyes, which you can never forget; by those last cries, that wrung your heart when you could neither help nor save; by the desolation of that empty cradle, that silent nursery, – I beseech you, pity those mothers that are constantly made childless by the American slave-trade! And say, mothers of America, is this a thing to be defended, sympathized with, passed over in silence?

Do you say that the people of the free states have nothing to do with it, and can do nothing? Would to God this were true! But it is not true. The people of the free states have defended, encouraged, and participated; and are more guilty for it, before God, than the South, in that they have *not* the apology of education or custom.

If the mothers of the free states had all felt as they should, in times past, the sons of the free states would not have been the holders, and, proverbially, the hardest masters of slaves; the sons of the free states would not have connived at the extension of slavery, in our national body; the sons of the free states would not, as they do, trade the souls and bodies of men as an equivalent to money, in their mercantile dealings. There are multitudes of slaves temporarily owned, and sold again, by merchants in northern cities; and shall the whole guilt or obloquy of slavery fall only on the South?

Northern men, northern mothers, northern Christians, have something more to do than denounce their brethren at the South; they have to look to the evil among themselves.

But, what can any individual do? Of that, every individual can judge. There is one thing that every individual can do, – they can see to it that *they feel right*. An atmosphere of sympathetic influence encircles every human being; and the man or woman who *feels* strongly, healthily and justly, on the great interests of humanity, is a constant benefactor to the human race. See, then, to your sympathies in this matter! Are they in harmony with the sympathies of Christ? or are they swayed and perverted by the sophistries of worldly policy?

Christian men and women of the North! still further, – you have another power; you can *pray!* Do you believe in prayer? or has it become an indistinct apostolic tradition? You pray for the heathen abroad; pray also for the heathen at home. And pray for those distressed Christians whose whole chance of religious improvement is an accident of trade and sale; from whom any adherence to the morals of Christianity is, in many cases, an impossibility, unless they have given them, from above, the courage and grace of martyrdom.

But, still more. [. . .] What do you owe to these poor unfortunates, oh Christians? Does not every American Christian owe to the African race some effort at reparation for the wrongs that the American nation has brought upon them? [. . .]

To fill up Liberia with an ignorant, inexperienced, half-barbarized race, just escaped from the chains of slavery, would be only to prolong, for ages, the period of struggle and conflict which attends the inception of new enterprises. Let the church of the north receive these poor sufferers in the spirit of Christ; receive them to the educating advantages of Christian republican society and schools, until they have attained to somewhat of a moral and intellectual maturity, and then assist them in their passage to those shores, where they may put in practice the lessons they have learned in America. [. . .]

O, Church of Christ, read the signs of the times! Is not this power the spirit of HIM whose kingdom is yet to come, and whose will to be done on earth as it is in heaven?

But who may abide the day of his appearing? "for that day shall burn as an oven: and he shall appear as a swift witness against those that oppress the hireling in his wages, the widow and the fatherless, and that *turn aside the stranger in his right*: and he shall break in pieces the oppressor."[3]

Are not these dread words for a nation bearing in her bosom so mighty an injustice? Christians! every time that you pray that the kingdom of Christ may

---

3   Refers to Malachi 4.1.

come, can you forget that prophecy associates, in dread fellowship, the *day of vengeance* with the year of his redeemed?

A day of grace is yet held out to us. Both North and South have been guilty before God; and the *Christian church* has a heavy account to answer. Not by combining together, to protect in justice and cruelty, and making a common capital of sin, is this Union to be saved, – but by repentance, justice and mercy; for, not surer is the eternal law by which the millstone sinks in the ocean, than that stronger law, by which injustice and cruelty shall bring on nations the wrath of Almighty God!

4

Further Reading

Further Reading

Recommended Editions and Further Reading

Elizabeth Ammons (ed.), *Critical Essays on Harriet Beecher Stowe* (Boston, Mass.: Hall, 1980).

Josephine Donovan, *Uncle Tom's Cabin: Evil, Affliction, and Redemptive Love* (Boston, Mass.: Twayne, 1991).

Leslie A. Fiedler, *Love and Death in the American Novel* (New York, N.Y.: Criterion, 1960).

Thomas F. Gossett, *Uncle Tom's Cabin and American Culture* (Dallas, Tex.: Southern Methodist University Press, 1985).

Joan Hedrick, *Harriet Beecher Stowe: A Life* (New York, N.Y.: Oxford University Press, 1994).

Ellen Moers, *Harriet Beecher Stowe and American Literature* (Hartford, Conn.: Stowe-Day Foundation, 1978).

David S. Reynolds, *Beneath the American Renaissance: The Subversive Imagination in the Age of Emerson and Melville* (New York, N.Y.: Knopf, 1988).

Shirley Samuels (ed.), *The Culture of Sentiment: Race, Gender, and Sentimentality in Nineteenth-Century America* (New York, N.Y.: Oxford University Press, 1992).

Charles Edward Stowe, *Life of Harriet Beecher Stowe, Compiled from Her Letters and Journals*. 1889 (Detroit, Mich.: Gale Research, 1967).

Harriet Beecher Stowe, *A Key to Uncle Tom's Cabin*. 1853 (New York, N.Y.: Arno, 1968).

Harriet Beecher Stowe, *Uncle Tom's Cabin*, ed. Jean Fagan Yellin (London: Oxford University Press, 1998).

Harriet Beecher Stowe, *Uncle Tom's Cabin, or Life Among the Lowly*, ed. Ann Douglas (Harmondsworth: Penguin, 1981).

Eric Sundquist, *New Essays on Uncle Tom's Cabin* (Cambridge: Cambridge University Press, 1986).

Eric Sundquist, *To Wake the Nations: Race and the Making of American Literature* (Cambridge: Belknap, 1993).

Electronic Resources

The most comprehensive Web Site is Uncle Tom's Cabin and American Culture, found at ⟨http://www.iath.virginia.edu/utc⟩.

Other sites include

Harriet Beecher Stowe, at ⟨http://xroads.virginia.edu/˜MA97/riedy/hbs.html⟩.

Harriet Beecher Stowe, at ⟨http://digital.library.upenn.edu/women/stowe/StoweHB.html⟩.

Index